ROSANNE MICHIE

Change Your Life

In 10 Minutes

How aiming low can give you a high!

Published by Brolga Publishing Pty Ltd
ABN 46 063 962 443

PO Box 452
Torquay Victoria 3228
Australia

email: markzocchi@brolgapublishing.com.au

National Library of Australia
Cataloguing-in-Publication data

Rosanne Michie, author. ISBN: ?? (paperback)

A catalogue record for this book is available from the National Library of Australia

Printed in Australia
Cover design and typeset by WorkingType Studio

BE PUBLISHED

Publish through a successful publisher
National Distribution to Australia & New Zealand
International Distribution to the United Kingdom

Dedicated to my incredible late mum, Effie, who taught me to never give up and how changing even one inch can make your dreams come true. To my proudest success story Raphaela and Romany, for whom change had to be mastered if we were to survive. To Michael, Finn and Zac for showing me that doing whatever it takes to change is worth the effort.

In many cultures the dragonfly is a symbol of change, transformation, hope and connection to a spiritual world.

It is also a reminder of Alex Preston, who lost his life to cancer when he was just eight years old.

Although I never met Alex, he inspires me every time I am fortunate to see a dragonfly — which is now part of my own story

— Rosanne Michie

CONTACT US

Join our *Change Your Life in 10 Minutes* tribe

Website:

www.changeyourlifein10minutes.com

Email:

community@www.changeyourlifein10minutes.com

Follow us on Instagram:

changeyourlifein10mins

Contents

A note from Rosanne:
Why me?

I was walking past a giant billboard the other day. It featured this beautiful woman, tousled bedroom hair, wearing nothing but a bedsheet.

"These sheets literally changed my life," she purrs in the advertisement.

Geez, if bed linen can transform your goddamn life, why am I shy about putting my own philosophy forward?

I am not a psychiatrist. I am not a psychologist. And I don't have a doctorate in do-gooding.

But I am a storyteller.

At the start of each chapter of this book, I'll weave in a personal story to remind you that we all have a history — some of it helpful, some of it horrible — that shapes us and influences our choices. Life-changing moments launch each chapter's theme, leading into lots of tips. Each of those tips in its own small — or huge — way has the power to create change.

Who am I to write a book dispensing advice (pointers that don't even have anything remotely to do with bed sheets)?

I have steered myself down some shitty one-way streets and had more than my share of head-on crashes. Yep, I've stumbled through failure, grief, pain, trauma — even terror. And I've had periods of great joy and happiness.

I am like you. I get stuck. I get caught in the "shoulds", excuses, dread, guilt, stuckness and slackness.

But to make something of my life and to shield my children, I have had to confront change, whether I liked it or not. Change is scary and uncomfortable at first, but there are ways to make it possible?

I also have a passion to see others survive and thrive. None of us wants to look back in 10 years and wish we'd done better.

Ten minutes is enough to shift your energy on a busy day when you don't have time for more.

And, I'm here to tell you, it works.

Introduction:
The 10 Minute philosophy

If time is money, we're all going broke.

We all want our lives to improve. But frankly, who has the time? And who can be bothered?

It's time to stop over-thinking and under-achieving. No more putting off jobs, dreams, hopes and goals, and no more getting stuck trying to do something perfectly or not at all.

Free yourself of the pressure of perfection. I have discovered that you really *can* get a high by aiming low.

We all procrastinate and get stuck in a rut sometimes. The longer it goes on, the more difficult it is to climb, lift — or scratch — our way out.

The hardest part of any action or change is getting started. Motion of any kind — even something that's not on our to-do list — will get us on our way. Staying put might feel safe, but being stationary either in our minds or bodies for too long is a slippery slope to stagnant and stuck.

Start small, create specific goals and don't wait for a right time. You'll be amazed how far change will take you.

If you want evidence that the 10 Minute philosophy works, look no further than this book. Whenever I got stuck as I worked on it (which was often) I researched and wrote it in 10-minute increments until it was done.

How to use this book to change your life

Change Your Life in 10 Minutes is packed with 10-minute tips in the form of doable, digestible bites. Consider them life snacks or hacks. Most are free or low cost. Pick one that works and repeat it every day — or chomp through the menu.

More often than not, if you commit 10 minutes to stretching, swimming, cooking, deep breathing, walking in nature, running, getting your "om on", dancing, decluttering — or even re-cluttering — you'll end up doing much more.

Ten minutes can turn into 40 minutes, an hour, 10 hours — 10 years.

But if it doesn't, 10 minutes a day is great. It is enough to begin to create genuine, lasting change by establishing the foundation for a daily practice. Creating positive change can be easy — if we have the right approach to adopting more good habits and fewer bad ones. (1.)

It's time to get unstuck and shift the blocks. Get moving. We only need the dial to shift one per cent for change to occur. All change starts with something small, and daily rituals are powerful. Small steps lead to giant strides. The smallest change can transform your life forever (2.).

Add 10 Minute tips to your day and watch your results multiply. They're all it takes to change your life.

Because you really **can** Change Your Life in 10 Minutes ...

This is a shame-free zone. Say goodbye to your inner critic.

No more blame-game beating yourself up for where you're at, what's going badly or how you're feeling.

You're in the right place. It's about choosing things you can do. Pick tips you love (or at least don't hate the most) and then do more of them. Stick to one or a few and make the habit a daily ritual. Or work your way through until you find something that feels like the right fit.

We all want change in some way — to be a better friend, a better parent or better child. To be nicer or kinder. To eat better, lose weight, look better.

To lose the addictions and destructive behaviour. Be more successful or healthier. Improve or maybe even end a relationship. Learn something new. Care more for ourselves. Be smarter. Get a better job. Be better at our job.

The disconnect between what we want and what we actually do is often a source of pain. Changing what we do, even in 10 minutes, can powerfully bring us closer to what we really want. It can bridge the painful gap between what we want and where we're at. (1.)

This book is not based on the belief you have to change. You're perfectly enough how you are right now. Besides, being perfect sounds boring. But if you want to make small or big changes, you're in the right place. This book will help you to shine even brighter.

You really can change your life in 10 minutes.

Bite-sized bits

"You are one decision away from a different life."

"Do it now, sometimes later becomes never."

"The way to become the person you want to be a year from now is to take small steps consistently" - Dana Marie Kirkland

"Growth can be painful, change can be painful, but nothing is as painful as staying stuck."

"If you have a heartbeat there's still time for your dreams." – Sean Stephenson

"I don't care what you do. Just do something." – Effie Michie

"What kept me sane was knowing that things would change, and it was a question of keeping myself together until they did." – Nina Simone

"Be proud of small accomplishments – never underestimate the power of your small wins." – Viola Davis, Academy award winning actress and philanthropist.

Chapter 1

I am stepping slowly into what feels like baby vomit. But dark. Dank. And icky.

It is as dreadful a morning as you could get in the depths of winter at 6.45am on one of Australia's most exposed, rugged and freezing coastlines in front of the aptly named Salty Dog Cafe.

I stand on the edge of the big chop, shivering alongside a few brave, disparate strangers calling themselves WOW, short for Wednesday Ocean Waders, whom I have connected with online in desperation. They are there to test themselves, splash about in the shallows and commune with nature. I am there to start swimming training.

Did I mention it was still dark?

I am not a swimmer, I should explain. Yet I have agreed to swim around an island in six months' time with friends who are capable and experienced ocean swimmers.

I hate missing out on anything, especially an adventure with after-exercise fun and food. So here I am.

The waders chatter, fuelled by the solidarity created by their shared goal — to just get into the water.

"I'm off to the buoy," I say, teeth chattering. I make sure I am still in their line of sight, for I know it's not safe to swim in the ocean on your own. Let alone in the dark. Let alone in baby puke.

My scrawny arms seem like toothpicks poking into the sizeable swell. I have the technique of a tractor with a flat tyre. Jerk, grind, jerk. And the buoyancy of a brick.

Somehow, I make it the 250 metres or so to the bobbing yellow float.

I don't know if it is the tide, but I seem to have momentum on the way back to shore. The sun is rising. There is a rhythm and hum previously unknown to my normal staccato strokes.

And then the magic happens. And it's in this moment that the idea for this book comes!

I had been feeling like complete crap. Scared. Reluctant. Hopeless at swimming. Old. Unfit. Foolish. Stuck.

After the relatively simple act of pushing through, my mood and sense of self are transformed. I feel FANTASTIC.

Yes, you really can change your life in 10 minutes. How?

By just giving it a crack.

1 — Water ... blue space

*"In time, and with water,
everything changes."*
— **Leonardo da Vinci**

We all know we can't live without water, but we tend to take its healing, restorative and survival qualities for granted.

Being near — and on, in or under it — can calm and connect us, spark ideas and insight, make us better at what we do and even help heal what's broken.

Neuroscientists are starting to tell us what real estate agents have long known about the value of a sea view — our brains are hardwired to react positively to water.

Most religions, with their symbolism around birth and rebirth and cleansing by rituals such as baptism, understand its power. Some Catholics even take it one step further by bottling it and labelling it holy water!

There are limitless ways to use water to heal, soothe, support, inspire — even to cure.

Water makes up 70 per cent of the earth's surface. It might be an ocean, river, creek, lake, mineral springs, swimming pool or puddle. Other times it could be as simple as your daily bath or shower that elevates a hygiene function to a significant salve and wellbeing ritual.

Stress affects how we function. Whenever we sense real or imagined danger our bodies kick into a high gear. Do we fight? Do we freeze? Do we flee?

Stress and its bedfellows, anxiety and depression, can literally kill you. Incredibly, one in two Australian women experienced mental illness in 2022, according to one study. [7]

The World Health Organisation has predicted that by 2030 depression will be the number one health concern in developed and developing nations. [3]

Quite simply, water can be used to wash stress away. And another bonus — if you're in it, there's nowhere to put your mobile phone!

Vitamin sea

Ways we know — swim, surf, sailboard, fish, snorkel, kayak, canoe, sail, paddle, wade, dive, float, skinny dip or boogie board ...

Cold-water therapy

An elixir for good health, cold open-water immersion has been linked to an improved immune system, pain relief, reduced inflammation, increased concentration and libido (!), endorphins and improved mood.

We're off to Vagus, baby!

Ever heard of the vagus nerve? It holds some of the keys to better health and happiness. Cold water triggers the vagus nerve, which runs from the neck to the abdomen and is in charge of turning off our response in terms of fight, fright, flight or freeze.

The deep breathing we need to do to get into cold water turns on the vagus nerve and switches off the stress response. (This is also why breathing mindfully in meditation makes us feel calm almost instantly.)

Understanding how to stimulate this nerve is a big step to opening our minds and helping us focus.

Inflammation damnation

So many diseases stem from inflammation in the body, including autoimmune diseases like arthritis, and depression.

We don't need science to tell us that if we immerse any part of our body that's inflamed and swollen in cold water, the inflammation reduces.

We cold-water swimmers feel an immediate high after our swim, and general mental and physical wellbeing in between dips also seems to improve.

But, as always, don't make any changes without the support of your health professional.

Top 10 Minute Tips to Change Your Life

1. **Get in, on or under the ocean or safe, clean waterways**

   Not everyone is comfortable stripping off and squeezing into a swimsuit. It's easier said than done, but try not to worry about what you look like

2. **Stand or sit by water**

   Close your eyes, breathe deeply and visualise yourself looking and feeling at peace

3. **Bare those feet**

   Take your shoes and socks off and walk in water

4. **Douse your face with cold water**

   It stimulates the vagus nerve — our body's communication highway and part of the parasympathetic nervous system — which helps slow the heart rate, relax the body and activate the metabolism

5. **Cold shower**

   Let the vagus nerve know you mean business! It sounds awful, especially in winter, but research shows taking cold showers can increase alertness, improve circulation, ease muscle soreness and reduce stress

   Getting bold with the cold. With both these hacks, start with 10 seconds and repeat, working your way up each day until you reach 10 minutes

   Start by slowly decreasing the amount of hot water you use in your shower and ease yourself into cooler showers. Once you've got the temperature that's right for you, enter the shower slowly and take a few deep breaths. Then start getting wet slowly with your hands, then feet, then the rest of your body

6. **Have a warm bath**

   Include Epsom salts, magnesium or essential oils. Light a candle and practise gratitude

   Try a bathtub meditation. Practising mantra meditation in water can enhance its impact as there is some evidence sound vibrations can add to the soothing effect. This, combined with the experience of being in water, can help relax the nervous system and relax intense emotions

Or try turning off the lights and having calm mantra music playing. Slowly begin to let go, releasing tightness in each part of your body and letting go completely. Allow your thoughts to float by without following them, as you would in meditation

This is particularly helpful during times of trauma, distress, anxiety, pain or if you feel overwhelmed

7. **Draw a cold bath**
    Dial things up a few notches by trying an ice bath or plunge pool

8. **Community and connection**
    Join a swimming or wading group (a shout-out to Torquay's Wednesday Ocean Waders and the Torquay Ocean Swimmers) or investigate other local groups

9. **Hydrotherapy**
    Water helps the body feel weightless and buoyant while providing natural resistance to movement, making it perfect for rehabilitation and fitness training

Water exercises can help tone muscles, increase range of motion, ease arthritis pain, improve joint flexibility, relieve muscle spasms, decrease inflammation, facilitate low-impact aerobic exercise to support weight loss, and speed recovery from injuries, allowing exercise to begin sooner than on land

10. Water aerobics

Don't knock it until you give it a try. It's fun, low impact and can be social. Do 10 minutes yourself with the boom box or use your 10 minutes to research and join a class

11. Play

Catch a wave in the ocean. Do bombs in swimming pools or deep water-holes. Try a few somersaults. Grab a boogie board or skiffle board

12. Learn to swim

Research has shown that babies and young children in swimming lessons from an early age are ahead on motor skill developmental milestones. As an adult, getting a few lessons can improve your water confidence and give you more options for your world in water

13.   Invest in a wetsuit and a proper swimming cap

It's not a competition. If a wetsuit or vest means you get in the water rather than opting out, do it. I can vouch for the relief from a neoprene cap

14.   Expectant mums

Water-based exercise can have a positive effect on expectant mothers' mental and physical health. There's research showing that the bub on the way also benefits

15.   Disabilities

Parents of children with developmental disabilities often find that their children love recreational activities in and around water. This can also improve family connections (see below)

16.   Drink water

Say no to that next glass of wine, cocktail or beer. If alcohol no longer serves you, stop drinking. Or reduce your intake. Your body, mind — and wallet — will thank you. Hydrate, particularly before and after caffeine or alcohol

17.   Japanese water therapy

Drink three-to-four glasses of water at room temperature when you wake each morning, then wait 45 minutes before eating. At each meal, eat for only 15 minutes, and wait at least two hours before eating or drinking anything else.

There are some claims (unverifiable but positive reports) that this can aid hypertension and diabetes, and, of course, proper hydration has numerous benefits. These include optimal brain function, sustained energy levels, and body temperature and blood pressure regulation. Drinking more water may help prevent constipation, headaches and kidney stones. (As always consult a health professional before trying. Drinking excessive amounts of water — or anything else — is never recommended)

18. **Listen to water**

    The sound of water balances, soothes and energizes, and can bring a feeling of peace and tranquillity. If you can't be sitting by a fabulous ocean, under a waterfall or by a babbling brook, research says you can get similar results from listening to a recording

19. **Schedule a sesh in a flotation tank**

    While there is a cost involved for a session in one of these tanks, floating helps lower cortisol levels. This relaxes the nervous system, alleviates pain and reduces negative effects of stress. The tanks are also known as sensory deprivation tanks, and the practice of using them is known as restricted environmental stimulation therapy.

Question: How do you get a beach body?

Answer: Take your body to the beach. Or the sea, the river, the lake — whatever the blue space — don't be concerned what shape your body comes in.

Nature comes in all forms and so do we.

Exercise

How to breathe when immersing yourself in cold water

1. Avoid the temptation to run and dive in. Walking slowly is better to maintain a steady heart rate and avoid sending panic signals to the brain

    ◆ As you step into the water, avoid the reflex to clench up and hold your breath. Breathe deeply — inhale and exhale gently

2. Regulate your breath as you immerse yourself in the water. In through the nose and out through the mouth, emphasising and elongating the out breath

3. Take your time. Breathe steadily, rhythmically and evenly

4. Start "box" breathing. Imagine a rectangle — two short ends at the sides and two longer ends on the top and bottom. Move your breath around the rectangle in your mind as you breathe in and out

   ◆ Starting bottom left, inhale for the count of two up the short side of the rectangle and exhale for the count of four as you visualise going across the long side

5. Work your way around the notional box until it's time to leave the water. It's a great way to distract your focus from the cold and bring calm and strength to the practice.

The Wim Hof method

Known as the Iceman, Dutchman Wim Hof previously held the Guinness World Record for the longest swim under ice.

His method, based on scientific research, focusses on three pillars of the relationship between water and wellbeing:

◆ Cold therapy (the "blue space" doesn't have to be the sea or a lake but can be a bucket of cold water or a cold shower)

- Breathing to reduce stress and boost the immune system

- Commitment to move from our comfort zone, particularly into cold temperatures

Hof argues that by learning to control our response to the cold we can train our bodies to better cope with physical stress, strengthening our circulatory system in ways that might affect cardiovascular health and help us gain some control over our immune systems

It's not easy and it's not for everyone. But the results can be amazing.

Exercise

- Take about 30 quick breaths, then exhale, keeping your lungs empty for as long as possible.

- When you are gasping for air, take in a quick breath and hold it for 10 to 15 seconds.

- Repeat this cycle three or four times.

(Don't use this method for swimming though, as there's some risk of passing out.)

Water and people with disabilities and special needs

My beautiful stepsons, Finn and Zac, love being in the water.

They both have autism and an intellectual disability — although their ability levels, personalities and needs are very different. They have a natural affinity with being in the ocean.

In the water, everything feels calmer. For many people with autism spectrum disorder, the noise, feelings and business related to the outside world finally stop. Water feels interesting, and the way light moves through it can be fascinating.

For children with autism, water offers resistance, pressure, comfortable temperatures and pleasant sensory arousal.

There's generally less social pressure and it's easier to ignore the world around you when you're so focused on staying above water.

It is an ideal environment for exercise and rehabilitation due to its constant temperature, buoyancy, density, pressure and resistance.

Water also makes the body feel lighter and relaxes muscles as it decreases stress. And that's just for the parents (joke)!

Did you know?

A thalassophile (n) is someone who loves the ocean.

Water activities for people with special needs can improve:

◆ Motor function — including strength, co-ordination, balance and endurance

◆ Sensory receptors

◆ Social skills

◆ Communication

◆ Cognition

◆ Emotional responses

◆ Aquatic skills and water safety.

Did you know?

Water has the ultimate power of constant change. When cold, it freezes and crystalises; when hot, it steams; when touched, it ripples. It makes up between 65 and 78 per cent of our body and more than 70 per cent of our brain, heart, skin, muscles, kidneys, lungs and liver.

Remember to always be safe around water. Our tiredness levels, mood, physical ability — even what we've eaten — can affect how we interact with it.

One of the joys of water is that no two days represent the same conditions. Ensure you're familiar with the situation before taking the plunge. Never swim alone.

While the curative effects of water are impossible to deny and there is plenty of anecdotal (and an increasing amount of scientific) evidence about the power of water to assist with addictions, anxiety and depression, these are complicated mental health issues, and any steps first require guidance from a health professional.

Don't do anything that makes you uncomfortable. Be gentle and listen to your mind and body.

Bite-sized bits

"Pure water is the world's first medicine."
— Slovakian proverb

"Water provides the most profound shortcut to happiness out there." — Wallace J Nicholls PhD

"Salt water heals all."

"Be like water. Flow, crash, fly."
— Md. Ziaul Haque

"Going into the water, you leave autism behind ..."
— Don King, whose son Beau has autism and swims with his dad

"If there is magic on this planet, it is contained in water."
— Loren Eiseley

"Water links us to our neighbor in a way more profound and complex than any other."
— John Thorson

"You never regret a swim."
— Effie Michie

Chapter 2

I remember the shrill of the phone splintering the late-night air. The huge old black Bakelite blower with its snake-like coil attached to the handpiece rattles with the vibration.

There are muffled voices. Despite the low mumbles, there is panic in the air. The phone screams again. Pressure mounting. Rumbles. More fear. The hum might not be loud but the intensity is deafening.

The dark of my room is fractured by a triangle of light as my bedroom door opens. My mum looks distraught but her voice is measured. And so, so kind.

I see her mouth moving and she is holding me tightly, but I don't remember any actual words until she says.

"Your dad ... he has ... died. You must be strong."

I am six.

Something about my young person's belief and optimism that anything is possible, including superheroes living forever, somehow transmutes "Your dad has died" into "There is hope".

My mum, Effie Michie, leaves the room, presumably to have the same heart-breaking talk with my siblings, if she hasn't already. While I'm the youngest of five, I'm not sure what the pecking order was that dark night in April.

What is it about kids that they feel they are somehow responsible for crises that enter their lives. It must be my fault?

What can I do to fix it? I will never forget kneeling by my bed and begging God with a passion, honesty and earnestness that brings tears to my eyes all these years later.

"Dear God, please, please, please make sure my dad survives. I promise with my whole heart that I will always be good. I will do everything I'm told. I will never be naughty. I will do whatever I am asked. I promise. I promise. Promise. Promise ..."

"Please don't let my dad die."

It took me weeks, probably months, to understand the horrific reality. I'd wake up euphoric. "It was just a dream after all. Dad is still alive!"

I can still feel the relief. Quickly followed by the dark, devastating, sick reality. Dad was gone.

Earlier that day in April, my dad, Wally Michie, had held me in his arms, for what would be the last time, out the front of our parish church, St Aloysius. His best mate's daughter was getting married.

Mum said he was tired. He was working at three jobs to support our not-so-little family of five kids. He had rushed home from the racecourse, where he was moonlighting as a penciller for a bookmaker, to mow the lawn before putting his tuxedo on.

At the wedding reception, there was a widow sitting on her own looking a bit lost while couples waltzed around the dance floor. Wally was one to ensure everyone was OK, so he dragged his weary but fit 50-year-old body over to ask her to dance.

In the middle of the dance, he collapsed. Effie, the love of his life, rushed to him and scooped his head into her arms.

She said he looked at her with such love but the devastating understanding that he was slipping away.

He died of a massive heart attack. Right there in my mother's arms on the dance floor. At a wedding. His kindness to one widow, somehow proved to be the baton passing to another.

2 — Resilience

***"Turn your wounds into wisdom."* —
Oprah Winfrey**

"Gee, 10 minutes isn't very long," lots of people said to me when I told them about the concept of this book.

One of many things I learnt that night as a six-year-old is that life can change on a dime.

My life changed in that one moment. So when one second is a lifetime, 10 minutes is infinity.

Somehow life without my dad goes on. But now, every single thing looks different.

I resolve to cram as much as I can into every day because I know too well that it can be over at any second. I learn, (for better or worse), to be strong, just as Mum had told me.

And I learn to survive, by developing what gurus are fond of calling *resilience*.

But what is it and where do you get it? I call it the ability to bounce rather than shatter. Or if you do fall apart, it's knowing where to get the glue to stick most of the pieces back together again. If you look closely, though, you can always still see the evidence of where the repairs have been made!

In Japan they've even turned it into an art form called *kintsugi*, which means golden repair. They put broken pottery pieces back together with gold to show that by embracing our flaws and imperfections, you create an even stronger, more beautiful piece of art.

The veins of gold show breakage and repair as part of the history, rather than something to disguise.

Resilience is our ability to respond flexibly to the cracks, crevices or crashes. It's our mental reserves of strength that help us handle stress and hardship. It's accepting that life is full of challenges. While we might not be able to avoid issues, we can be open to adapting to change.

The good news is that resilience skills can be learned. The bad news is — it's frequently the hard way! Resilience is often born of pain, disaster, grief, trauma, stress or other challenges.

World Health Organisation figures show we in the West are more depressed, less connected, more anxious and more likely to die by suicide than ever before. (3)

The figures are chilling.

In 2017-18, one in five Australians — 4.8 million people — reported a mental or behavioural condition. After COVID, the prevalence of mental health challenges, especially anxiety and depression, has spiked to what medics have called the shadow pandemic.

In Belgium, France, Italy, Mexico, New Zealand, the United Kingdom and the United States, the prevalence of anxiety in early 2020 was double the level of previous years.

Anyone who is close to someone struggling knows the wider impact of distress — the circles of suffering that ripple outwards to friends, mums, dads, brothers, sisters, workmates.

If ever we have needed survival skills and resilience, it is now.

Top 10 Minute Tips to learn resilience

1. **Hello, I'm here. Speak up and ask for help**

   Consult a health professional, psychologist or counsellor. Speaking to a professional can really help you get out of your head and work out some concrete next steps

   Speak to a friend. It's different to speaking to a dispassionate professional, but good friends are the best

   Even just 10 minutes reading about people who have experienced and overcome similar issues can motivate, support and inspire

   Online communities can provide support and be a place to talk about issues with people who have been in a similar situation. Tip: Do your homework and make sure you trust the community before becoming embedded

Attending support group meetings can be a great — and sometimes life changing or saving — way to talk about your challenges and to find a network to provide compassion, support and role models

2. **Find your tribe. Connect with the right people**
Welcome people into your life who value you and whose values you share. Avoid negative, toxic and "can't do" people who always have a reason why things won't work

You don't need everyone to like you. And you can still be a kind person and not like everyone

3. **Love yourself sick (to become well.) Take care of yourself**
Invest in yourself. Take 10 minutes a day (or even a week) to look inwards to reflect on what you really want and value. This is always time well invested

4. **Deal with your shit**
We all have a history that includes emotional wounds, and it influences our choices. If you're not happy with your responses, work through your issues. See above, work with a supportive professional

5.   Clean the lens. Focus on what's going well

I talk more about gratitude later, but foster a habit of noticing what's going right, rather than what might be going wrong. Think about what you can do, not what you can't. Appreciate the small things

6.   Right here, right now. Be present

Reflecting on the past and goals for the future is great, but also concentrate on the here and now. Don't let the worst of the past or fear about the future dictate your present

7.   Sack the cynic. Remain hopeful

It takes courage to be hopeful in a world that can be brutal, but maintaining hope is vital. Behind every success story is a series of failures and stuff-ups. Learning from them leads to resilience

8.   Be the boss of you. Take charge of your own health

Feeling your best, mentally and physically, is so important in building resilience

9.   Find your happy place

Surround yourself in nature, get in the water, join a club, find something you love to do and do it endlessly

10. Get outside your comfort zone

Do something each day that scares you. It doesn't have to be extreme. Try a new hobby, speak to the barista at your local coffee shop or call someone you haven't spoken to for a while. Anything outside of your comfort zone that makes your stomach turn just a little is what you're aiming for

11. Hug it out

Touch is vital. Hugging someone releases oxytocin, the happy hormone which can lead to relaxation, trust and compassion

12. Pat an animal

Pets have a powerful impact on reducing our stress and promoting healing

13. Say cheese

Emotions are contagious. You may be pissed off, hungover, unhappy at work or going through a tough time, but simply smiling makes you — and the next person — feel better.

Play your way to resilience in 10 minutes

Our brains are hardwired to remember negative events and information. It's called *the negativity bias*. If you're having a stressful day, or trying to sleep, odds are that your brain will be replaying those stressful events long after the stress has passed

So "change the channel" by playing a mental game

You can count backwards by seven starting at 1,000, recite song lyrics, create a sentence where every word must begin with the same letter, starting with "A" For example, "All animals are awesome." Then go onto "B". "Big bucks buy boats."

Don't forget your meds!

Meditation — Practise being calm each day, breathe (tips in Chapter 6)

Exercise — At least 10 minutes of physical activity every day (tips in Chapter 11)

Diet — be mindful of what food is fuelling your body (tips in Chapter 10)

Sleep — good quality sleep is one of the most powerful ways to reduce stress and depression while increasing energy, memory and learning.

10 Minute purpose reflection activity

....

Get a pen and write down your responses to:

* Why do I bother getting up in the morning?

* What keeps me awake at night?

* What does being successful look like?

* How can I apply my gifts to something that excites me and helps others?

* When am I most alive and lit up?

* What can I do to make a difference in one person's life, today?

* What is my elevator pitch (if you summarised your purpose in one sentence, what would it be)?

- If I say yes to living aligned to my purpose, what do I need to say no to?

- If I met a younger version of myself, what advice would I give me?

- What mark do I want to leave?

Top 10 Minute Tips
to change your life

Tips for building resilience in children

- **The village**
  Show your children the importance of connecting with friends and peers, having care and empathy. Encourage catch-ups with friends and appropriate use of phones, video, texts and other tools

- **It's not all about me**
  Encourage them to help others and to contribute. Try age-appropriate volunteer work or ask for help yourself with tasks they can master

- **Get in the groove**
  Sticking to a daily routine can be comforting and reassuring for children, who flourish with structure in their lives

- **It's a jungle out there**

  Take a break. Social media, online, the TV news or even what's happening at home or in the playground can be scary and trigger upset. Build in unstructured time during the day to allow children to be creative, active or be still. Show them simple breathing or meditation techniques

- **Play is powerful**

  Show your child the importance of basic self-care like making time to eat properly, exercise and get enough sleep. But make sure they have time to still be kids, have fun and do stuff they love

- **Dare to dream**

  Support them to have attainable dreams and goals and show them that moving towards those dreams and goals is a process undertaken one step at a time

- **I am who I am**

  Instil a positive self-image. Remind your child how they have successfully handled hardships in the past. This builds strength and confidence for future challenges. Help your child learn to trust their instincts to solve problems and make good decisions

- **Life is 10 per cent what happens to you and 90 per cent how you react to it.**
  Keep things in perspective. Even when your child is facing painful situations, help them look at the broader context. It's hard for kids to see past today, but explain that things change and the future can be good

- **Yada yada yada. Talk!**
  When they have questions, answer honestly. Let them know you're there for them. And that you love them no matter what

- **Change is hard at first, messy in the middle but fab in the end**
  Change is scary for everyone. But the more kids can see they are safe, surviving or even thriving as a result of change the more resilient, adaptable and open to further change they'll be

- **Yee har! Let's party**
  We are often quick to notice things that are not working or things we are not able to do, and this can limit our progress. By celebrating small (and big) victories each day we can keep our motivation high.

Try this exercise: write in your diary at least one thing each day that you consider a small or great success (of any kind, not only things related to your school or work). You may have cooked something delicious, helped a stranger or listened to a friend... After having written about your success, pat yourself on the back and find a way to celebrate it. Be creative.

Resilience and teens

If you are parenting teenagers or are a teenager, I have two words for you: Shit Show.

Probably the best thing you can do is take note of good old former US president Abraham Lincoln, who said: "This too shall pass."

Saddle up because emotions are volatile and close to the surface. It's a time of confusing duality for teenagers and their parents. "I don't want your advice."/ "Please help me." "Leave me alone."/ "Where are you? I need you?" "I hate myself."/ "I am so damn shit hot."

Or the most common: "F*ck off."/ "I love you."

Resilience tips for teenagers

1. **Feels like home**

   Find a place your teenager can create as their safe space — their bedroom or somewhere they find comfort. Get used to the door being closed. Make sure you knock and respect boundaries by not bursting in

2. **Let them come to you**

   There's a lot of driving teenagers around these days. I found the car was a good time to let conversations flow organically. Let them control the music on the radio

3. **The best way to recharge is to unplug**

   Online bullying is rampant. Put safe practices in place. Encourage time away from connectivity. No phones at the dinner table

4. **Without creativity there's no progress**

   Encourage art, writing, journaling, music movement like dance, and other exercise as outlets

Lose "poor me", say hell-*oh* boss

If you're dealing with a crisis, see yourself as a survivor instead of a victim waiting to be saved. Look for ways to resolve the problem. Being a victim can become a part of your identity.

The "poor me" or helpless child is learned behaviour and can be changed. I truly get that your situation may be dreadful or unavoidable, but there's still a path to a positive outcome.

It's normal to be unsatisfied, distressed or feeling injured in some parts of our lives, but there's always a bigger picture.

- Think about what's troubling you

- Remind yourself that suffering is part of being human

- At this precise moment many other people are facing their own challenges. Some might even be facing the exact same challenge. There is a common humanity

- Be kind to yourself. Use the same language and compassion you would towards a friend. Phrases like "It'll be OK", "I'm here for you" and "I care about you" can be helpful

- Take 10 minutes to visualise taking the reins and steering yourself out of the rough

- Pat yourself on the back; you've become the agent of your life, your own boss woman (or man)

- Repeat the mindset as often as you need.

Bite-sized bits

"Grief and resilience live together."
— Michelle Obama, Becoming

"Turn your anxiety into action. The best way to deal with a crisis or life is to build resilience, it's a muscle."
— Sarah Wilson

"Fall down seven times, stand up eight."
— Japanese proverb

"A good half of the art of living is resilience."
— Alain de Botton

"It's your reaction to adversity, not adversity itself that determines how your life's story will develop."
— Dieter F. Uchtdorf

"Do not judge me by my success, judge me by how many times I fell down and got back up again."
— Nelson Mandela

"I can be changed by what happens to me. But I refuse to be reduced by it."
— Maya Angelou

"Rock bottom became the solid foundation in which I rebuilt my life."
— J.K. Rowling

Chapter 3

If I close my eyes, I can still hear the sobbing …

For a while after Dad died there was a sort of elevated but unnatural atmosphere. Even though life was so far from ordinary, everyone, especially Mum, was busy trying to put on a normal face and get through, to show what was expected of a regular rhythm of life.

Whatever regular was supposed to look like for a solitary middle-aged woman with two mortgages, five children under 16, school fees to pay, no job and no family support.

"We're going to be OK," I heard her repeat. They were the words she was saying, but even though I was just a little kid, I knew she was anything but.

The mood felt like stretched elastic on a pair of dirty old undies that are two sizes too small. It was holding up, but the tension could snap at any time, resulting in a flood of embarrassment, shame, judgment and failure.

If I'm honest, the little extroverted me rather enjoyed the constant ring of the doorbell, with well-meaning neighbours or parishioners, one after another, dropping in a casserole for the family in need.

That old black telephone worked overtime as friends from afar checked in.

People rallied around. Even though there was a weird, brittle vibe of unreality, there was also nervous excitement. People were very kind. Checking in on Mum.

"Is there anything we can do?" "Please tell us if we can help?" "We're here if you need us."

Despite the excitement and adrenalin, I remember feeling strange and outside my body, in a dream-like state. It was as if I was physically going through the motions and my head and heart were watching from above like separate entities.

As weeks turned into months the penny eventually dropped that Dad had gone.

And he wasn't coming back.

After three months — I remember exactly how long because Mum explained to us later that the three-month milestone is a crucial time in the grieving process — the shock wore off and the reality hit with the force of a fist to the face.

Mum — the strongest, most resilient, determined and selfless person I have ever met — cracked.

It was a double blow. Dad's loss had been the sucker punch, but dropping the bundle was the K.O.

The doorbell stopped ringing. People returned to their own lives and challenges. To the outside world Mum was coping amazingly. Later she spoke about that time and believed she had experienced a full-blown nervous breakdown.

Somehow, she still managed to keep the ship afloat. Kids were kitted out in freshly starched uniforms, lunch boxes were filled, meals were on the table. But inside, she felt broken.

My room was next door and I'd hear the strongest person I've ever known softly sobbing. She cried so hard and for so long I thought she was going to die too. I can still remember walking into her room and standing by the bed.

If I close my eyes, I can still see her lying crosswise, her face contorted with grief, on the bed she had shared with her beloved husband.

The sadness I felt in that moment is real even today.

Like all kids, I wondered what I had done to make her so sad and what I could do to make her better.

I could feel her pain. And I vowed at that moment to always try to be kind.

3 — Kindness, empathy & change

"Sometimes it takes only one act of kindness and caring to change a person's life."
— Jackie Chan

The golden rule of change is kindness.

We've all been told to treat other people how we like to be treated, be kind and respectful, and that kindness matters. But maybe we would have more incentive if we better understood the role of kindness in making helpful changes for ourselves as well.

Kindness is central to the 10 Minute philosophy because the smallest gesture can change a life.

And most of the time it doesn't cost us anything. Just a few minutes of our time.

When we extend kindness to those in need, we also somehow shift something in ourselves. When we help others, it can promote changes in the brain that are linked with our own happiness.

Kindness is the thing that connects us all. And, as US activist and poet Maya Angelou says, people might not remember what you said, but they'll never forget how you made them feel.

Make kindness a daily habit. If we take the time to be kind to other people, it pays emotional dividends.

If we are feeling vulnerable or struggling, doing some good can give us a more positive outlook on our own circumstances, which is a far better springboard from which to launch the life we want.

An act of kindness can build confidence and give us a sense of agency, happiness and optimism.

Kindness is also contagious. It can inspire others to repeat the good deeds and create a powerful ripple by paying forward what they have received.

Unexpected kindness is one of the most powerful, least costly, and most underrated agents of human change. And every act creates a ripple.

Good for our health, not just our emotions

Kindness has been shown to increase self-esteem, empathy and compassion, and improve our mood. It can decrease blood pressure and cortisol, the hormone which impacts our stress and adrenalin levels. Kind acts increase the serotonin and dopamine in our brains, which give us feelings of wellbeing. People who give of themselves in a balanced way tend to be healthier and live longer.

But what can I do?

Campaign for kindness to be built into business decisions, government policy, health support systems, schools and other areas in a way that supports mental health and reduces discrimination and inequality. But, as the cliché goes, it starts with one person. There's no such thing as an insignificant act of kindness — it all counts. So pay it forward.

10 Minute kindness tips

Kindness 101

1. **Small things, big impact**
    A smile, nice word, an unexpected deed, or a planned surprise

2. **Start with 10 minutes**
    Make kindness a daily habit

3. **Work to your strengths**
    Do something you enjoy. It's contagious

4. **Be my guest**
    Ask someone who'd benefit from joining you as your guest for an activity. It might be a social or sporting outing, a walk, a catch-up with family or friends — even just a chance to grab a coffee

5. **Pay it forward**

   While grabbing your morning coffee, pay for the person behind you as well. This simple act might inspire them to pass along some good in the world too

6. **Leave a letter**

   Carry around a stack of sticky notes. If you're feeling inspired, write an encouraging or complimentary note and leave it on your colleague's computer screen, or a family member's door or fridge

7. **Mentor**

   Offer your skills for those who may be struggling in a particular area. Share your talents via video call — you could teach guitar, dance or a new recipe

8. **Check in**

   Look out for a neighbour or acquaintance who might not have family or friends nearby

9. **Spoil 'em**

   Baking some biscuits or buying treats to share with your colleagues can be a mood booster. Take a few minutes to chat

10. **Praise a parent**

    If you see a parent under pressure, tell them they're doing a good job. If their kid is acting out at the time — even better. It's stressful and other people's negative judgment hurts. Most parents rarely hear how well they're doing

11. **Say cheese**

    If you see a stranger taking a family photo, offer to snap the shot so everyone can be included in the moment

12. **I see you**

    Take the time to learn the name of someone who regularly helps you out — the security guard or cashier at your grocery store, a cleaner at work. Introduce yourself and greet them by name

13. **Manners maketh the (wo)man**

    Remember to show respect by saying hello, please, thank you etc.

14. **Learn how to accept a compliment**

    I don't know about you, but I'm crap at accepting compliments. If you don't know how to respond, say: "That's so kind of you." It shows appreciation without you feeling like you're completely up yourself

15. Honour the offer

None of us wants to make anyone feel like a loser or self-conscious by drawing attention to a problem or need. But politely asking "Is there anything I can do to help?" could be more powerful than you may know

16. Give

It could be time, money or skills. The spirit of giving enriches us and helps us better understand how we fit into the world around us

17. Well done, you

Open up your inbox every morning and send at least one email to someone in your network or circle praising or thanking them for something they have done or achieved.

Be real, not perfect — self-compassion

Many of us respond with kindness and understanding for others yet beat ourselves up when we stumble ourselves. Treat yourself with the same kindness and compassion that you extend to loved ones when they fall.

Self-compassion exercises

1. Think of a situation that is troubling you

2. Take 10 minutes to write a self-compassion letter

3. Stand up to your inner critic

4. Lose the "could have, should have, would haves". Accept the way it is

5. No matter how guilty or responsible you feel, forgive yourself

6. Write for 10 minutes a day in a self-compassion journal.

"En Oh" — there. You've said it!

Because kindness means sometimes putting other people's needs before our own, how do we learn to say no and still be a good person who helps people?

The answer is to put healthy boundaries in place. And then stick to them.

There's no value in running yourself ragged and putting yourself second.

You are of more help to others if you are firing on all cylinders.

How do I learn to say no and still be a nice person?

Automatically saying yes to other people is different from being kind to others. Being able to say no is one of the kindest things you can do for yourself. And it can also liberate the people who maybe lean on you too much.

Most of us like to be liked. And it's great to have a can-do attitude and help people where we can.

But saying yes all the time can lead us into people-pleasing territory, which is also known as TNPA — The Nice Person's Abyss!

Exercise

- **Tip:** Take 10 minutes to work on supporting phrases to give yourself a little time to get the clarity to say yes or no.

- Setting healthy boundaries means you can be more generous with your time. If you're not run down, stressed and over-taxed, you have energy for people and projects you value.

- Remember, saying no doesn't require explanation.

Ways to buy time to not say yes (or no) in the moment

- Let me come back to you on that

- Give me 24 hours

- I'm not sure I'll be able to swing that. Leave it with me.

Bite-sized bits

*"A part of kindness consists in loving people
more than they deserve."*
— Joseph Joubert

*"Before you abuse, criticise and abuse,
then walk a mile in my shoes."*
— Elvis Presley

*"Carry out a random act of kindness, with no expectation
of reward, safe in the knowledge that one day someone
might do the same for you."*
— Princess Diana

"Be kind whenever possible. It is always possible."
— His Holiness the Dalai Lama

"Always be a little kinder than necessary."
— James M. Barrie

*"A kind gesture can reach a wound that only compassion
can heal."* — Steve Maraboli

*"If you want others to be happy, practise compassion.
If you want to be happy, practise compassion."*

Chapter 4

I am living in a swanky place in a really nice suburb.

Never in my wildest dreams did I imagine that love could lead me here. However, it's not the luxury I'm referring to but something sinister. True love has acquired a death rattle.

I have two beautiful young daughters, Raphaela and Romany. Things are probably looking rosy from the outside. Inside, it's tense, toxic and emotionally unsafe.

There are certainly lots of good times. The highs are very high. But these are accompanied by episodes of fear, unpredictability and the undercurrent of always walking on eggshells.

It may be a beautiful house, but it is not a happy home. The situation is escalating at the same time as the health of my beautiful, beloved, and now ageing mum, Effie, starts to deteriorate. She doesn't have much time left.

My head is in a vice and my heart feels as tight as tennis racquet strings. I am constantly fighting back tears and holding my breath. A boa constrictor is twisted around my chest and it's squeezing hard.

I am too scared to exhale for fear my whole life might unravel.

Mum, the most incredible person I've ever met, eventually passes away. She fought and fought and fought until the end.

It's agony. My biggest fear has finally found me.

She was 87 and it was her time. But, of course, that doesn't make it any easier.

4 — Fear, anger & shooting yourself in the foot

"Don't let the fear of failure stop you trying new things. Life's saddest summary is: could have, might have, and should have."

I hate it when gurus and self-help books say: "You have to face your fears."

It may well be true, but it's just such an awful thought. What, bury myself among 100 poisonous, hungry snakes? Let them slither all over my face? Why would I want to do that?

But I have found, when we are up against resistance or a block — like inching into the ocean when it's freezing, for example — and we push through, something does shift.

When we face the big stuff such as surviving trauma, broken and toxic relationships, addictions, illness and injury, the blocks can feel more like a concrete wall.

A bit like the wall Donald Trump started to build on the US border to keep the Mexicans out — it might not make sense but the message is clear. Keep out. Don't push this boundary.

But it is the act of moving that generates the energy that enables us to navigate out of our comfort zone and past emotional roadblocks. The more we do to nudge the boundaries with tiny steps, the more confidence we have that we can make change and do the hard stuff.

This creates a positive brain pattern that sets us up to succeed. (The science of neuroplasticity and the brain's response and adaption to fear, stress and depression is fascinating. There's plenty of information out there if you want to do your own research and delve deeper.)

It's all very well to tell someone to stop being scared and just have courage.

For the person terrified of being on their own, scared of flying or getting up a ladder, or even afraid of letting someone else see their emotions or frailties, the fear is real.

It's uncomfortable and potentially crippling. People will do almost anything to not feel pain or discomfort.

Fear triggers the "freeze, fight or flight" response, which releases cortisol and adrenalin, and stimulates blood flow. The response is basically designed to enable an evaluation of "Do I eat it, or does it eat me?" in the space of .85 milliseconds.

It's heavy shite!

Face those fears

What's the answer? Baby steps. Start with the discomfort around the edges. Think about the analogy of dipping your toe in the water. Breathe. No judgment or shame. You've done well. If 10 minutes is too long, start with 10 seconds. The next day or time, inch a bit closer.

Or, if you're that sort of person, just dive in headfirst.

Here's the thing. While we try so hard to avoid what scares us, there's research that shows we are subconsciously pulling ourselves towards our fears. We attract not only what we love, but also what we fear.

It's so unfair, but the woman who is scared her husband could be unfaithful ends up getting cheated on, the person terrified of being adrift loses their home, the guy who fears losing his dough ends up going broke, etc …

What we focus on grows. It's a law of nature. So, focusing on your fears without confronting and processing them can create the precise thing that scares us.

But fear gets a bad rap. It is essential, after all, to our survival. Fear is what prevents us walking in front of a bus or stops us diving headfirst off a cliff into shallow water.

It's how we approach it and how we let it influence us that matters.

If it's for a healthy change and you are ready, feel the fear and do it anyway!

10 ways to face — or fight — our fears

1. **Take time out**
   It's impossible to think clearly when you're flooded with fear or anxiety

2. **Breathe through panic**
   It's the last thing you feel like doing, but it helps

3. **Look at what's frightening you**
   Don't sugar-coat things. Honesty has power. If it's too scary, bring it back a notch but congratulate yourself for getting this far

4. **Picture the worst**
   Then work your way back and change the image, picturing a different outcome. See yourself smiling

5. **Look at the evidence**
   Logic can be soothing

6. Don't try to be perfect

You are good enough just as you are. Accept that you're doing your best, and that's great

7. Visualise a happy place

It can give you the perspective that this too shall pass

8. Talk about it

This can help externalise fear and get it out of your head. Listen to someone else's take on the situation. If it's crippling or a full-blown phobia, pick up the phone or get online and make an appointment with a professional

9. Count to 10

There's a reason why your mum said that. Sometimes 10 seconds can change your life too!

10. Have faith

It doesn't matter where you sit in terms of religion, spiritually or the universe, have faith that there's a process at play. Remember all the times you've succeeded. Believe in yourself. You're f*cking incredible.

Faith, belief and confidence

- Sit in a quiet place, relax and take five deep breaths

- Remember 10 tricky situations you've navigated

- Write them down. Put them on your phone. Turn them into a piece of art Turn them into a poem. Frame them.

Professional help

If you are facing serious challenges such as trauma, family violence or mental health issues, seek professional help. These 10 Minute tips can still be helpful for facing big issues, as they are based on taking one positive step. But in crises, speak to someone you trust and always consult a health professional.

Instagram perfect: It's bullshit

Somewhere along the way, we adopt this negative belief: "I am what I accomplish."

Research shows perfectionism often sets us on a path to depression, anxiety, addiction and life paralysis (5). Or maybe you don't need academic research. Just hop onto the 'Gram for 10 minutes if you want to feel like you're failing.

This paralysis by analysis relates to all the opportunities we miss out on because we're afraid to do something that won't be perfect.

It's the dreams we don't follow because of our fear of failing, making mistakes or being judged harshly by others.

It's terrifying for a perfectionist to take a risk, because it's their self-worth on the line.

I hate to tell you but despite what you might be seeing on social media, perfection doesn't exist. It is an unattainable goal. So better to start doing the best you can at this moment.

Tip

- A healthy version of striving to improve is: *"How can I improve?"*

- A perfectionist's version is: *"What will they think?"*

Shooting yourself in the foot: Self-sabotage

How many of us feel truly worthy of positive and healthy change? I too have sabotaged dreams with some deep-seated but erroneous belief I am not worthy of amazing things and must suffer as a "penance" for prior screw-ups or good fortune.

I'm all for shooting for the stars, but often we set our goals way too high in the beginning and lose patience or focus when the progress is slow.

But making small steps towards those goals whatever the kind of change we wish to make is usually much healthier, sustainable and productive in the long run than rushing to make several sweeping changes all at once.

It is also important to be real and set goals we know we are committed to and able to attain, even if it means asking for additional help and support. (1)

We can't expect everything to go our way or to happen overnight. Hoping for the best while being prepared for challenges and being gentle with ourselves is a great way to approach any type of change.

One of my lessons is, if I don't believe it can happen, it's not going to happen. And EVERYONE deserves happiness.

Loving yourself: self-confidence and belief

Let go or work around that inner worry of *what will people think?* Like the tennis player with the winning mindset, it's time to play your own game.

Exercise for self-confidence

Hello, I remember you! Revisit your victories

Strengthen belief in yourself by reflecting on past success you've had and the sticky spots you've wrangled your way out of.

If your brain rushes straight to the flops, remind yourself that failure and mistakes are natural learning opportunities. Let go of "old stories of ourselves".

Drop the judgment and comparisons. Even just being here in this moment is a sign of victory.

Same-same, but different: Comparisons

Comparing yourself to others is the thief of joy, according to a 2022 study by Liptember (7).

It's trying to simultaneously fit in and stand out.

Social media has given us an unparalleled but curated and filtered view into other people's private lives. Everyone else seems to be living their best life. Ah, the pressure.

Let's encourage each other to open up about our experiences and situations — positive and negative — without stigma. Limiting social media consumption can also help.

Remember that social media is a highlight reel, not reality, so let's not compare our lives through a flawed lens.

Exercise for releasing negative patterns

Bad habits be gone

Meditate for five minutes in the morning and five minutes at night

Q. Ask yourself: *what can I let go of in this moment, this week, this month that will support me to feel worthy of great things?* (It could be a decision, a pledge to let go of your own reactivity, a grudge you are holding. Or certain fixed views, attitudes or expectations that no longer serve you but you are holding onto.)

Cracking it, pissed off, losing it

Anger. We all have it and we each have our own triggers, often when we feel threatened, attacked, powerless, misjudged or frustrated.

Anger *can* give us movement and energy. But it's often messy as we don't usually act very skilfully when we act IN anger.

And we sure have very different ways of managing our anger. It's a fine balance striking the right level between unrestrained or open aggression — "all over the walls" type of anger — and swallowed-down, passive aggression, or repressed anger.

If we're angry, experts tell us the best approach is assertive anger. That means thinking before you speak, being confident but open and flexible to the "other side". It means being patient and not raising your voice; communicating how you are feeling emotionally and trying to understand what others are feeling.

Yeah, good luck with that! (Fair to say I'm still a work in progress ☺) At least we know what we're aspiring to …

Anger and irritability activate our nervous system and take a toll on our mental and physical health. They can lead to low self-esteem, substance abuse, relationship problems and plenty of regret.

But anger can be a good thing sometimes. It can give us a way to express negative feelings or motivate us to find solutions to problems.

Don't buy into the feeling that being afraid or ashamed makes you weak or wrong. Everyone feels these things sometimes. We are often afraid to admit that we are afraid, but anger, fear and aggression aid in survival. Without them, we die. So they are not useless.

It doesn't matter how it presents, and regardless of how we regulate it, our anger *is* trying to tell us something. But — as with everything — we need to be listening.

10 Minute tips to deal with anger

1. **Kaboom. Ouch**

   Punch a cushion or go one step further and invest in a boxing bag and gloves

2. **Rebel yell**

   Shout it out, but in a safe and solitary place. If you've been bottling something up and there's a particular a-hole — scream their name and what you want to say to them. The more expletives the better, frankly. (Obviously it's helpful if there's no one in earshot.)

3. **Write from the heart**

   Jot down what's pissing you off. Then ask: "What's *really* pissing me off."

   It's surprising that if you dig a bit and repeat the question several times, often a root cause will surface and you realise the thing that made you angry was just a trigger related to something deeper.

No need to be nice here. Dump the anger onto the paper to release it from your mind. Continue writing until you feel the anger releasing its grip.

If this insight doesn't come naturally, try speaking to a friend or a professional first

4. Unclench those teeth

We clench our jaws when enraged. Breathe through it and release those gritted teeth

5. Walk it out

Or if you're up to it, go for a run. Breaking a sweat really helps

6. Ease it out

Stretching is another key to unlocking the angry mind. It relaxes tightened muscles and improves oxygen flow to the brain, helping you think more clearly

7. Get your om on

Experts recommend going Zen and I know it does work, but sometimes when we are full of rage or resentment it is super-hard to tap into that inner peace

8. **Swing it sister**

   Tennis or golf are great. They take longer than 10 minutes, but anything that swings the shoulder, including chopping wood, is a proven rage reliever. This dates back to caveman days apparently, when raising the club was an essential part of self-protection by hunting, fighting or choosing flight

9. **Give yourself a good talking to**

   Tell yourself: "This is going to be OK!" Ask if this is going to matter 10 years from now. Most likely, the answer is no

10. **Where can I sign?**

    Sign up for an anger management course — there's some good stuff online and some are free of charge.

Bullshitting yourself — cognitive dissonance

Cognitive dissonance is a mouthful of big words but what does it mean? It's when someone holds two opinions/ideas/attitudes/beliefs that are inconsistent with each other.

For example, "Smoking is a stupid thing to do as it could kill me." And, "I smoke a packet of cigarettes a day."

We humans engage in all sorts of cognitive gymnastics to justify our behaviour. These thoughts and the resulting behaviour can limit our growth and lead to self-sabotage. But this is where guts comes in.

Choose courage over comfort. Be brave and invite new information to the table. Sit with it. Question. And, hopefully, become friends.

10 Minute tips to address cognitive dissonance

- Sit down with pen and paper or a keyboard and take notes

1. Practise mindfulness. Often we are unaware of cognitive inconsistencies. What conflicting attitudes come to mind?

2. Challenge your beliefs. The next step is to try to identify the cause of inconsistencies in your thoughts and, in turn, your behaviour and choices

3. Look at other choices

4. Discuss beliefs and the contradictions with a wise, kind friend. Or write them down and look at them from another perspective

5. Observe if there's any change

6. Repeat the exercise regularly until you feel you have made progress.

Bite-sized bits

"Feel the fear and do it anyway."

"I had a lot of worries in my life,
most of which never happened."
— Mark Twain

"Too often, we allow fear, worry, and doubt to dominate
and define our lives. We allow them to steal our joy, our
sleep, and our precious dreams."

"Sometimes the best revenge is to smile and move on."

"If you are patient in one moment of anger,
you will save 100 days of sorrow."
— Chinese proverb.

"Just because you're angry doesn't mean you have the
right to be cruel."

"You either get bitter or get better. You either take what
has been dealt to you and allow it to make you a better
person, or you allow it to tear you down. The choice does
not belong to fate, it belongs to you."
— Josh Shipp

"There is no innovation and creativity
without failure. Period."
— Brene Brown

"It's only when you risk failure that you discover things.
When you play it safe, you're not expressing the utmost
of your human experience."
— Lupita Nyong'o

Chapter 5

What almost nobody knows is that behind the picture-perfect home in the fancy suburb, the glamorous parties, international sporting events and the wholesome kids' activities, things are unravelling. Scarily.

Life is playing out to a backdrop of episodes of family trauma.

Out of respect for loved ones, I won't detail the specifics. Suffice to say, it becomes clear that despite all our best family values, hopes, dreams and intentions — and a crippling, suffocating fear that is gripping me — I must find the courage to move. Even one little inch will equal victory.

It is clear that I must create a new, steady, optimistic environment for my two beautiful kids and myself.

At least I have a good job, I tell myself. So many women in my position are not as fortunate.

I get paid handsomely as a newspaper columnist, a gig that's coveted by colleagues for its profile, reward, front-row seat at sporting and social events and flexibility to work from home.

Thanks to the incredible kindness and generosity of my close friend Moley, who lends me the money for a house deposit while I untangle the complicated threads, I am fortunate to be able to create a new, stable home.

Life is full of upward swings and downward spirals. And we never quite know where we are on the cycle.

Just when things are starting to look up, sharks at work start to circle. My column is axed. I've been shafted and I am out of work. No income protection. No Plan B. Three mouths to feed.

My options are limited as I know I need to be around for my girls. The big-paying jobs demand long hours away from home, which would make it impossible to be anything like the parent they need and deserve. Just when it feels like I might be moving forward, I realise I am in a bad jam.

Here I am. Stuck. A rock and a hard place. Wedged.

5 — Blocked. Stuck in a rut? It's time for change

"It's never too late to start over. If you weren't happy with yesterday, try something different today. Don't stay stuck."

Big dreams start small.

Once I get past the crippling fear of the unknown and the changes which are required, I try to see what survival and liberty would look like. From where I am positioned — in the little emotional ball I've curled myself into — it is hard to make out the definition.

You wouldn't call it a vision, more like squinting through shattered glass to glimpse a tiny glint of possibility and sunshine.

I realise that agency and self-efficacy — my belief I am able to manage what needs to be done — can come if I break things down into small, manageable steps.

It is always easier to walk along a path that is well worn from being gone down before. Even though we might really want a new direction, starting a new path in a field of tall grass is much more uncomfortable and does require more motivation and energy, a fact that can be a huge roadblock.

But if you feel stuck in a rut and can't get yourself moving, that's OK. I have come up with a foolproof solution.

I call it "inching".

If you can't find the way to run, walk. If you can't walk, crawl. And if you can't seem to move at all — and we've all been there — try inching.

Just one inch. Just 10 minutes. Just move a little.

Creating momentum means doing a little something to move us forward and a little less of the things that hold us back. Some days progress feels like an inch, while other days it feels like a mile.

Longer-term goals are important but it's less scary and more doable to set our priorities and plans in bite-sized chunks. Choosing one thing to work on at a time focuses our attention on things that are manageable.

Listen to that little voice in your head to make change that is right for you.

Start small, create specific goals, and don't wait to get started. You'll be amazed how far change will take you.

Someone told me once not to fear failure; fear being in the same position this time next year.

There will never be a perfect time to start. There are always reasons not to. Accept your time is now. Sometimes when things are falling apart, they might actually be falling into place. As the sportswear brand tells us: "Just Do It!"

Get moving. Inch by inch, mile by mile.

But how?

1. Let go of the judgment, shame, self-sabotage and quest for perfection

2. Start small

3. Start now. It doesn't matter what you do, just do something.

Procrastination is best put off until tomorrow. Kidding. Start right now

Do you sometimes go to bed feeling really pumped to make a change in your life, but by the time you wake up you find yourself falling back into old patterns?

We are wired for immediate gratification. Long-term consequences — even though we might really want them — can't compete with the here and now. Get me the results today. Right this minute.

Procrastination is not the same as laziness or a lack of willpower. People in a lazy space simply don't do anything and are fine with that. People who are procrastinating, on the other hand, have the desire to do something but just can't seem to start.

Not only do we avoid what we're supposed to be doing, that avoidance also blocks us from everything else we want to do. We put off doing anything at all, spend a ridiculous amount of energy thinking about it, feel guilty but still avoid what we're supposed to be doing.

Instead, we might leave it to the last minute, stare at the wretched wall, eat chocolate, blow time on social media or do a little cheeky online shopping.

Don't confuse procrastination with relaxation. Being peaceful and reflective recharges us. Procrastination drains us. The less energy we have, the more stressed, depressed or stuck we become and the higher the chance of us putting off our responsibilities, priorities and the fun bits that follow.

As you have already worked out, being stuck is often more painful and frustrating than tackling whatever it is we are avoiding.

The problem is not doing the work, it's *starting the* work.

We've already talked about fear triggering the "freeze, fight or flight" response. If we have evaluated a threatening or challenging situation such as facing a big (or small) task and if we haven't bolted and we haven't flown into battle, we're left "stuck right there".

We're rooted to the spot. Or maybe we're just rooted.

There is a myth that motivation just kicks in as a result of passively reading something inspirational or downloading an app on how to manage your time. But motivation often only comes *after* starting a new behaviour or task, not *before*.

And when the time is right for you, it is easier to change than to stay the same.

Rituals: the pre-game routine

Have a look at any of the world's top tennis players.

Watch how they prepare to serve. The number of times they bounce the ball. The way they might mop their brow with the back of their wristband. Fiddle with their shirt, hair or face. These are not mindless ticks.

Think of Raphael Nadal and his rituals, which included wearing both socks at the exact same height, towelling off after every point and picking out his wedged underpants from his shorts every time before he served?

Rapha has corrected assumptions that his rituals were a result of obsessive compulsive disorder (OCD).

"It is a way of placing myself in a match, of ordering my environment to match the order I am looking for in my head. It's a routine. When I do these things, it means I'm focused, I'm competing ...," he said.

The magic of a ritual or a pre-game routine is that it provides the pattern or a way to start what we want to do. It gets us in the right headspace. And it makes consistently following through easier.

It's like mental shorthand that takes away the pressure of having to make a decision. *How do I start? When do I start? How the hell do I do it?*

It propels us into action.

Most of us don't get moving because we can't work out how to get started. We overplay the impact of one defining moment and underestimate the value of small daily improvements. We put pressure on ourselves to make some earth-shattering enhancement.

The key to a good pre-game routine is it should be so easy that we can't say no to it. It shouldn't take massive muscle or motivation.

For example, my writing routine starts by making a cup of tea or coffee. When sitting at my desk doing a job that I'm hating, I religiously write the time down on my notepad.

Then I promise myself I can stop after 10 minutes. My meditating ritual starts by lighting a candle. These tasks are so easy, I can't say no to them.

If you're physically moving or engaged, it's much more likely that you'll feel energised. Have you ever danced to a song you love and not felt alive, engaged and energised? I haven't.

By the way, physical movement doesn't have to mean exercise. If your goal is to meditate every day, for example, then your routine should bring you closer to the physical act of meditating.

The one percenters

Improving by one percent isn't particularly notable — it isn't even *noticeable* — but it can be far more meaningful in the long run.

We only need the dial to move one per cent for change to occur.

In Australian rules football, their impact is so significant that "one percenters" are now officially recognised as a statistic. They are tiny efforts that may not individually affect the outcome of the game but collectively can change the overall performance of the team.

The difference a tiny improvement can make over time is potentially life-changing. Someone who is much better at maths than me wrote that if you can get one percent better every day for a year, you'll end up thirty-seven times better by the time you've finished.

The science: Newton's First Law of Motion

Newton's First Law applies to how we form habits. Things that are in motion tend to stay in motion. Once a task has begun, it is easier to continue moving it forward because there is a natural tendency for a moving object to keep moving.

Nearly all the friction in a task is at the beginning. After you start, progress happens more naturally. So, it is often easier to finish a task than it is to start it.

Exercise

Take 10 minutes to reflect: Where are the one percenters I can make in my life starting today?

If we want to achieve success or get a job done, we must create momentum.

So get moving! The key to getting motivated is to make it easy to start.

Tap into our power or agency

Stuckness can often make us want to wallow in helplessness. Identify an aspect of your life where you don't feel in control and then do something about it. You can't be stuck and in motion at the same time. So taking 10 minutes to do something strengthens our ability to get unstuck.

Three easy tips that build self-efficacy or choice over our lives

- Decide what you want for dinner

- Send out one job application

- Phone a friend

Follow your instincts

It is through science that we prove, but through intuition that we discover, or so the saying goes. Listen to your instincts.

Going to war with yourself — dealing with limiting beliefs

One of the things that stops us the most from moving or changing is a clash between our values.

In my case, it was a conflict between the deep belief that marriage should be forever and that problems should be dealt with in the family unit versus my values that a person's liberty and safety are paramount.

What to do?

Our beliefs drive our behaviour. If we want to adopt a new habit to drive change, these old beliefs can start to get in the way. Values which have helped us so well in the past may no longer serve us.

Remember, it's never too late to start over in life. Just one inch. Just 10 minutes. Just move a little.

Top 10 Minute Tips for Change

1. **Have a good hard look.** If you want a different outcome, work out what you need to change. What are your beliefs? What's your purpose? What does happiness or survival or success look like? We are creatures of habit, so look at your negative patterns. Then, peek inside to see if you can find insight into what may be driving these repeated issues

2. **Do something different today**

   ◆ Routines have their advantages but when you change an aspect of your behaviour, it effectively rewires your brain to make new connections

   ◆ Do things with your less dominant hand

   ◆ Take up a new hobby

   ◆ Take a different route or method of commuting into work

3. **Hello day.** First thing in the morning is a good time to start — but it doesn't work for everyone. Experiment with what works for you

4. **If they can do it, so can you.** Look for success stories and people who have changed and done what you are dreaming of. Seeing that others have once been where you are now and accomplished change helps you achieve it

5. **Make a list.** For people to change, they need to buy into the belief that the change is necessary. List the potential benefits

6. **Kindness, always kindness.** Don't be too hard on yourself. Change usually takes time. To change an ingrained, unhealthy habit into a new, healthy behaviour can take over three weeks of repetition (and sometimes a lifetime) before it sticks

7. **Knowledge is power.** Read books, scour websites, listen to podcasts, follow the right people on Insta, be open to new ideas and inspiration. Yep, it takes longer than 10 minutes (but maybe you can do it in small chunks), but reading autobiographies of people who have overcome insurmountable odds can give us perspective and confidence

8. **What's the plan, Stan?** You need a plan of attack, a step-by-step process. This is why 12-step programs are so successful. We don't simply walk into a meeting, change and be cured. But the structure lays out a process that works for many

9. **Hope is not a strategy.** Commitment is needed to make real change. For example, if you want to change how you deal with anxiety, seek out therapy methods. Stick with the plan until the change process is complete. Just hoping the anxiety will simply go away is not a plan

10. **Log on.** Look for dedicated online support forums and Facebook groups. There's a wealth of helpful information out there, but be sure to only rely on credible sources

11. **Log off.** The barrage of information is coming to us in a million byte-sized pieces. This blitz of information and social media can be mind-numbing and disturbing. Delete social media from your phones and turn off notifications

12. **Get uncomfortable.** Enter new territory and step out of your comfort zone. Your mind and habits will be resistant to change. But start with 10 minutes

13. **Find people who understand.** Don't underestimate the power of partnering with others on the same path. When you're dealing with a new transition, it's good to talk to a trusted person

14. **Mono-task.** We may think we get more done by multitasking and it may look like we're busy, but the reality is that "mono-tasking" — just focusing on one thing at a time — is more productive in the long run

15. **Look after your mental health.** Major (and minor) life changes can influence our decision-making process and increase feelings of anxiety and depression

16. **Lighten up.** It's easier to change your habits if you're enjoying yourself, so make it fun.

Exercise

The 10-minute change hack

Every day straight after waking up (and giving thanks for at least three things) pick one task, set your iPhone timer for 10 minutes, and work on that one thing non-stop. You'll be surprised how much you achieve. And, who knows, that 10 minutes might run much longer ...

Exercise

Habit stacking

Remember when your parents told you to turn around when you leave a public place and check the table and chairs to make sure you haven't left anything behind?

It turns out they were ahead of the game in terms of a change technique called "habit stacking".

It's when you partner a new thing you want to do with another habit already integrated into your daily routine. For example:

- After I pour my cup of coffee each morning, I'll meditate for one minute

- After I take off my work shoes, I'll immediately change into my workout clothes

- After I sit down to dinner, I'll say one thing I'm grateful for that happened today

- When I see a set of stairs, I will take them instead of using the lift

- When I walk into a party, I will introduce myself to anyone I don't know yet

- When I want to buy something over $100, I will wait 24 hours before purchasing. (Note: Don't do it! ☺)

- When I serve myself a meal, I will always put veggies on my plate first

- When I buy a new item, I will give something away — the one in, one out rule

- When the phone rings, I will take one deep breath and smile before answering. (1)

Exercise

Planning can be fun

Take your aspirations, dreams and goals and break them down into tiny behaviours. No matter your artistic ability, sketch the outcome or chart the steps or stages. Start now. It's fast. It's free. It's effective.

Exercise

The morning ritual

We know, we know ... that lil old pandemic has left its mark on some of our habits, including that extra time in the cot.

If you're working remotely, avoid the temptation to roll out of bed and straight to your computer. For some of us, this manoeuvre might only be a matter of metres as the screen takes pride of place next to your washing basket and wardrobe!

- Take 10 minutes to walk outside in the fresh air if possible. Breathe, stretch, set an intention for the day of one thing you are going to do more of, one thing you are going to let go

◆ If your body feels like it, try a five-minute jog or sprint. Follow it with a five-minute ritual, as above

◆ If nipping out isn't possible, lie or sit and practise some mindfulness. If you have the space, find somewhere else other than your bedroom, which may already double as your office/yoga studio/love nest.

Stuff you can do in 10 minutes that will change your energy

◆ Go for a walk

◆ Prepare a quick healthy meal

◆ Phone a friend

◆ Read a few pages of a book

◆ Do something creative

◆ Listen to a guided meditation on YouTube

◆ Text friends

◆ Take a power nap

◆ Some self-care — a quick face mask, light a candle, stretch

---

- Google chakra cleanse. Close your eyes and do a quick scan

- Give your wardrobe a quick tidy-up. Take out at least five things to give to charity

- Listen to a few of your favourite songs.

Skills you can master in 10 minutes
(It's great for your brain as well as your life)

- Learn a simple song on the guitar

- Learn how to read someone's palm

- Learn how to order your meal in another language

- Learn how to say hello in 10 languages

- Learn how to make perfect scrambled eggs

- Brush up on first aid

Bite-sized bits

"The secret of getting ahead is getting started."
— Mark Twain

"Before Alice got to Wonderland, she had to fall."

"Only by changing your thoughts
will you change your life."

"I've never met a strong person with an easy past."

"Success is a few simple disciplines, practised every
day; while failure is simply a few errors in judgment,
repeated every day."
— Jim Rohn

"It's not more time you need. It's more quality use of the
time you already have."
— Alan Cohen

"We are all broken. That's how the light gets in."

"Tomorrow is not promised and today is short."

"Listen to your intuition. It will tell you everything you
need to know."
— Anthony J D'Angelo

"Don't wait for the perfect moment. Take the moment and
make it perfect."

Chapter 6

My girls and I need some fresh air, a bit of fun and perspective while I work out a plan for our future. I pack up the car and head to an Easter country tennis tournament.

Although tennis played a huge part of my early life, I haven't been playing regularly due to all the confusion, commitments and conundrums. But I get on the Aussie grass courts and there's no dampening that fierce competitive spirit. It feels fantastic.

"I'm back!"

I play match after match as organisers try to push through the program on day one. I'm weary but in some ways energised. As I serve, I put my weight on my left foot but suddenly feel a stab of pain in my calf, like I have been shot. My leg crumples underneath me. I'm lying face down on the grass and can't get up.

I've snapped my Achilles tendon.

The symbolism is not lost on me. In Greek mythology the Achilles heel is a metaphor for a fatal weakness despite overall strength.

Mum has just died. I already lost my dad years ago. My marriage has broken up. The trauma and damage has been profound. The girls and I are still healing, trying to put the broken pieces back together. I have just lost my job and I have no income.

And now I can't walk.

All of us have our rock bottom moment. This is mine.

You can change your life in 10 minutes. Mine just changes, for the worse, in one second.

How the f*ck are we going to survive?

So all these years after that dark night in April when my dad died, here I am. A solitary middle-aged woman with school fees to pay, no job and little available family support.

If we look closely, there are always patterns around our behaviour and experiences. It is obvious that history is repeating a bit. Mum found herself at the abyss and worked out how to feed five kids. I do feel guilt and shame as her situation was absolutely no fault of hers. Mine, I feel, is the consequence of some poor decisions.

But I am fortunate to not have a mortgage, and two kids are much easier to feed than five, I reason. I don't know how I am going to do this, but we are going to survive.

In Mum, I could not have had a better role model of courage, strength, grace under pressure and survival.

The doctors tell me it's a 12-month injury and I would have been better off had I just broken the leg. I can't drive for months. Can't even make a cup of tea as I am unable to carry it with crutches. I have to crawl on my belly up the stairs to my bedroom, dragging the plaster-encased offending limb in my wake.

A pattern I inherited is always trying to do everything myself. Why is it so hard to ask for help? One of many humbling lessons for me is to learn that the only way out of this bind is to graciously accept assistance.

The principal and parents from the girls' school — some I don't even know very well — organise a roster to ferry them to and from. Grant, a very nice man I have started dating , is so supportive. He helps by doing the shopping, bringing me wine and chocolate and keeping me company.

My friend Moley rallies round and makes me laugh at the abject grimness.

Another lesson I learn is it's very often not the people you've helped in the past who step forward and offer a hand. Ironically, it's those with no debt to settle.

I will never, ever forget the kindness of those people who came to our rescue. I can't imagine where we would be if you hadn't bothered to put yourself out. It's thanks to you that we survived and that we flourish today.

And. Every. Single. Day. I am Grateful.

6 — Gratitude, mindfulness & breath

"Appreciation can make a day, even change a life."
— Margaret Cousins

The first thing I do when I get up every morning — as soon as my feet hit the carpet — is take a deep breath in and out and give thanks for at least three things.

(Actually, if I'm completely honest and not giving you too much information, I start this way and then normally need to pee, which interrupts my spiritual awakening.)

One of the things I'm most grateful for is that the challenges and my ultimate survival story has made me more appreciative, not less. I am blessed. The furthest thing from a victim.

What separates privilege from entitlement is gratitude, the ability to focus our energy and attention on what we have rather than what we don't have, according to author Brene Brown.

And I found that gratitude and mindful breathing is what liberates us from self-preoccupation.

There is overwhelming evidence that a simple gratitude practice can transform chaos into order and confusion into clarity. It can make sense of our past, bring peace today and create a vision for tomorrow. And regulating our breathing consciously is one of the best things we can do for our wellbeing.

Positive psychology researchers tell us that practising gratitude has a significant impact on our wellbeing. Grateful people have stronger immune systems, are happier, deal with challenges better, are more generous and forgiving and feel less isolated.

Bloody hell, for that return, why wouldn't we all spend 10 minutes? So, these days my attitude is gratitude.

I just read that a baby smiles between 50 and 70 times a day, and a toddler about 600 times (10.)

Look around you. So many grumpy faces … your boss and workmates, your partner, the person serving you at the checkout, friends, relatives …

Where the f*ck have those smiles gone?

The other thing I notice about babies is the way their bellies rise and fall with each breath. So many of us shallow-breathe, particularly when we're stressed or hunched over a computer.

Am I the only person who finds it a bit shocking that — rather than progressively developing — in some areas we are regressing from the moment we're born? Fundamental instincts that we are all born with like smiling, proper breathing, a sense of joy and living in the moment, have to be re-learnt.

The good news about brain science is that it turns out you *can* teach old dogs new tricks. The landscape of the mind is an endlessly fascinating place.

The buzz word is "neuroplasticity", which means we can change the structure of our adult brains and our behaviour at whatever age we are by focusing our intention. (If you're interested in more detail, there's heaps of good reading on neuroplasticity.)

We can create new neural pathways that lead to better choices and happier feelings. It's not too late to learn new tricks.

The most effective, immediate — and cost free — way we can reduce our stress levels is to focus on our breathing. Not only will it change our lives, it can save our lives.

Post pandemic, a staggering one in two Australian women were experiencing mental ill health, according to research (7.) Meditation, mindfulness and deep breathing as an antidote might sound like woohoo, hippy trippy nonsense but they are firmly rooted in neuroscience.

Taking several deep breaths cuts signals to the brain and allows what's known as the parasympathetic nervous system to do its job.

Consciously regulating our breathing is one of the best things we can do for our wellbeing.

In positive psychology research, gratitude is strongly and consistently associated with greater happiness. Gratitude helps people feel more positive emotions, relish good experiences, improve their health, deal with adversity and build strong relationships.

The three Ps of perspective

If something bad happens, find perspective by asking yourself:

* Permanence (Will this last for ever?)

* Pervasiveness (Does it affect all aspects of my life?)

* Personalisation (Am I to blame?)

What's the time? Now o'clock

Too many of us engage in the *if* and *then* model of happiness. *If* I buy that new car, *then* I'll feel happy. *If* I find a partner, *then* my life will be good. *If* I lose weight, I'll be happy *then*.

If you keep waiting for the big moment when you can make that change that will lead to happiness, well, you're wasting your time. Our ability to feel happier comes from inside ourselves, not from external circumstances. The happiest people have found a way to live in the now. So there's no time like the present to make the decision to feel happy and grateful, no matter how tough things might be.

Tips

- Make peace with your flaws. Give yourself permission to be imperfect

- Make room for imperfections in others too. (BTW this is different from settling for a bad situation)

- Let go of unrealistic expectations

- Appreciate and be grateful for what's good in your life now

- Keep life interesting by trying new things and using the 10 Minute philosophy

The busy-ness beast

There's a fine line between living a full, interesting, purposeful life and being too busy.

When I overload my schedule, these days I have to stop and ask myself: *"What is it that I am avoiding?"*

Sometimes we do several things at once to prevent boredom, avoid something difficult or uncomfortable, or crowd out the thoughts so we don't have to look at the things that are blocking us.

Tips

Break down your tasks and activities over an average week

- Look at the things you do that aren't adding value to your life

- Are there any tasks you use to "hide behind"?

- What can you let go of?

GEM exercises

Gratitude

- Write down: What are three things that went well for me today?

- Write down: What am I looking forward to most about tomorrow?

Empathy

- Think about someone you know who is going through a hard time. Write down what you would say to them. Then pick up the phone, send a text or email to show them you're thinking of them and here to lend an ear.

Mindfulness

◆ Go for a walk and think about three things you can see, three things you can hear and three things you feel.

◆ Write them down.

Thanks to the Resilience Project for these exercises

Exercise

Make a gratitude list

Establishing a gratitude practice really can improve our lives. Not only does it allow us to live more in the present, but if we do it regularly enough, we'll find ourselves looking at things in a different way and searching for more things to be grateful for.

Make the first thing you do every morning a mental (or written or spoken) note of at least three things you are grateful for.

Another easy way to do this is to write down three good things that have happened to you in the past 24 hours. Also give some of the gratitude apps a go.

- Repeat it every day, or even a few times each day

- Watch what happens — abracadabra

Mindful breathing

We take 20,000 breaths a day, including while we are asleep. How many of those are we conscious of?

Even three minutes of mindful breathing can transform your life without spending a cent or using complicated equipment or programs.

Instinctively, we all know the benefits of taking a few deep breaths before or during stressful moments. Our breath brings oxygen to our brains and body, creating a sense of peace. It:

- Calms the stress response

- Strengthens attention

- Promotes brain integration

- Fosters better sleep

- Strengthens self-awareness

Mindful breathing practice

* The process of mindful breathing is simple. All you do is focus on your breathing. As one breath ends, so the next breath begins

* Many of us breathe shallowly with only the upper part of our lungs. The more stressed or excited we become the shallower we breathe. Filling our lungs from the bottom up — just as infants do — energises and relaxes us

* In a world that demands instant gratification it's normal to expect instant results. But be gentle and know that some days it's easier than others. Hang in there

* What strengthens the brain is not the length of time that we do the practice but the frequency

* All it takes is three minutes of mindful breathing a day to create change. That leaves seven minutes to do something else in the 10 Minute scheme of things.

Kick-arse mindful breathing exercise

If you've been feeling less focused, more scattered, or being reactive this technique really helps:

- Sit in a chair or on the floor with your back straight

- Breathe in for a count of four, hold your breath for a count of seven, then exhale for a count of eight

- Repeat this for five minutes. (The first few times I tried it I was all over the shop, but I've got the hang of it)

- The four-seven-eight method is a simple breathing exercise

- Begin by breathing in through your nose for the count of four

- Hold that breath for seven seconds

- Exhale slowly from your mouth for the count of eight seconds

- Repeat.

Mindfulness and meditation

What even is mindfulness?

Interchange the word "mindfulness" with "awareness". It's about paying attention to the choices we make rather than living on autopilot. This gives us clarity and helps us step away from some of the complexity.

Mindfulness and meditation are closely related but they are not the same. Mindfulness describes the state of *being* while meditation refers to the practice of intentionally increasing awareness to quieten the mind.

You might ask if we are even capable of being still without our hand darting for our phones? But don't you wonder who we could be if we paused more?

There's no wrong way to meditate; just make the time.

Top 10 Minute Tips

1.   Be present

Bring your attention to what you're doing in the moment. A trick to help your brain be present is to repeat in your head what you're doing right now: "I'm making my breakfast." "I'm opening my book to read." "I'm walking along the beach." The theory is if you learn to become an observer of your thoughts and not be overtaken by them, you'll spend less time struggling

2.   Let go of the judgment

It's hard not to put your own spin on it but try not to judge your thoughts as good or bad. Just acknowledge them

3.   Look for the good in the bad

Remember the silver linings

4.   Create routine

One way to live more mindfully is to structure your day to find your natural rhythms

5. **Bedtime**

Ditch the phone by your bed. After turning the light out, reflect for five minutes on the things that went well today

6. **Create a space**

- While we can do mindful breathing anywhere — in the car, on a bus, even in the bathroom — it sometimes helps to create a dedicated, comfortable space where you're unlikely to be interrupted

7. **Open or shut case**

Your eyes don't need to be closed but keep your mind in the present

- "Monkey mind", a Buddhist term meaning unsettled or restless, is normal

- Don't be hard on yourself. Every time your mind attaches on a thought, gently release it and return to your breathing

- If you're not sure your breath is right, place your hand on your belly and breathe deeply until it rises and falls.

10 Minute daily mindfulness meditation

- Sit in a comfortable position in a chair with a tall, straight back and rest your arms gently

- Close your eyes and bring full attention to this moment. Settle in and allow your mind and body to be still

- Bring your awareness to your breath. Take a deep breath in and then release it fully. Allow your breath to feel natural and easy as it flows in and out of your body. Do not try to force or regulate it

- When thoughts drift into your mind, allow them to float out

- Scan down your body, concentrating attention from body part to part

- Bring your attention to the top of your head and scalp. It might feel tingling or hot, with throbbing or soft vibrations. There might be strong sensations, or you might not feel much at all

- Repeat and focus your breath separately on your forehead, face and jaw; neck and throat; shoulders; down the arms to the wrists, palms and fingers. Then focus on your chest, observing the rise and fall of each breath. Then the upper and lower back; abdomen; and pelvis. Scan your legs, observing your thighs, knees, shins and calves, ankles, feet and toes

- Let them all relax and make them soft

- Sink into the state of relaxed awareness

- Take a moment to notice how you feel

- Bring your attention back to the room. Wriggle your fingers and toes. Slowly open your eyes

- Carry this state of peace into the day.

10 minutes of grateful every day

Take a moment

* Breathe in for a count of five, breathe out for a count of five. Repeat until calm

* (This is a helpful rebalancing technique, particularly in times of stress or anxiety — before walking on stage, entering a meeting, making a phone call)

* Jot down five things for which you are grateful in life

* Write down five things you do well. Note three things that have gone well today and why they went well

* If you are feeling frustrated or angry, write down what you are angry about followed by what you are grateful for. It's a powerful tool to unlock the angry mind.

The Law of Attraction

Our thoughts attract our results, as what we think about and believe, we tend to do. Our actions then produce the results. Limited and negative thinking leads to limited action, or even counter-productive action, and produces negative results.

Bite-sized bits

Sometimes the most important thing in a whole day is the rest we take between two deep breaths. – Etty Hittlesum

"This is a wonderful day I have never seen this one before." – Maya Angelou

"The heart that gives thanks is a happy one, for we cannot feel thankful and unhappy at the same time." – Douglas Wood

"If the only prayer you said was thank you, that would be enough." – Meister Eckhart

"We must find time to stop and thank the people who make a difference in our lives." – John F. Kennedy

"Be happy in the moment, that's enough. Each moment is all we need, not more." – Mother Teresa

"When I started counting my blessings my whole life turned around." – Willie Nelson.

"Sometimes when things are falling apart they might actually be falling into place."

Chapter 7

I am so excited but incredibly nervous.

My tennis is coming along nicely. I've quickly progressed from lessons and winning the beginners trophy at the age of nine by beating my dear friend Paulie S at the local church tennis club to playing proper tournaments.

Tennis is saving my life, giving me somewhere to stream my unbridled energy. Bashing the shiz out of that little fluffy ball is an incredible antidote for the grief of losing Dad and feeling like I am different to the other kids and don't quite belong.

I'm 12 years old now and have just joined a much bigger club where there are lots of kids with the same love of the game and dreams of grass court stardom.

Tennis is a family sport — and indeed the bloodline runs through mine. My dad, Wally, was a good A Grade club player. Mum and Dad met at the local club. When

Wimbledon is on, I am allowed to stay up till all hours and watch the old grainy black and white TV, even though I can't ever really see the teeny, blurry white ball.

But coming in as the youngest of five kids, I am the only Michie to pick up a racquet.

Most of the other aspiring players have brothers and sisters also playing. These are times when there is normally only one family car. So Mum, Dad and the kids all pile in and off to the courts it is …

But it's just me and Mum.

One of the things I love about tennis, even today, is the huge social element. It might be war on the court, but off it we all sit down and break bread; drink cups of tea or cordial; eat fluffy cream sponges or sausage rolls followed by Twisties and red snakes; and play cards or table tennis when it's raining.

There's an early flush of hormones. I'm one of the youngest but it's all starting to happen around me — the boys are flirting with the girls and the girls are pretending they aren't interested.

Mum and I hear about a selection coming up for a regional talent squad.

"You're only 12 so don't get your hopes up. You'll be one of the youngest trying out and there are only a few spots. You still have plenty of time."

The day comes and I have never been so excited or nervous. My hand is shaking so much I can hardly hold the racquet.

They ask us to hit and are rotating players in and out. It feels like I am on a stage being asked to sing and open my mouth and nothing comes out.

My forehand is a bit of killer, if I say so myself. I get a nice easy ball.

"Oh yeah, I'll make this a goodie." Wham!

But I'm trying so hard I overplay it dreadfully and slam it into the back fence. I suppose I manage to play a few nice shots, but all I can think of are the clangers.

One of the other girls, I'll call her Jane Brown, has been having some good results. She's won a few tournaments.

I'm a tiny thing, relying on speed and determination. But Jane is much bigger and has far more power. (Mum calls her a bit of a lump. Because in those days there was no law *against fat shaming. BTW she wasn't fat, just not really a natural athlete.)*

I'm pretty sure Jane will get in the squad. I am crestfallen because I look around and make a mental note of who will and who won't. For the handful of spots, I don't think this is going to happen for me.

Jane has an older brother I'll call Steve — who is a few years older and the ringleader of all the tennis kids. Mr and Mrs Brown are there too, of course. They know everyone. The Browns are part of the inner tennis sanctum. The In Crowd.

I get on well with them all despite my insignificance.

I've practised with Jane a few times. This was fortunate for me because it is unspoken but understood: Jane is better than you.

My name is called out. The head of the selection panel talks about looking for potential, instinct and athleticism rather than rankings.

I feel a surge of happiness and pure joy. Oh my God. Wow.

Weirdly, Jane misses out.

I am a bit embarrassed and ashamed as the whole Brown family greases me off. I'm too young to know that my good fortune really has nothing to do with her.

So, I feel guilty. There are tears from Jane, anger rumbling. Dark looks in my direction. I hear my name hissed tersely under breath.

Mum and I take off. She's rapt. So proud. She has big dreams. And so do I.

I remember the shrill of the phone splintering the afternoon air. That huge old black Bakelite blower with the snake-like coil attached to the handpiece rattles with the vibration. Again.

"Is that you Rosanne?" A pubescent boy, pretending to put on a high voice, is surrounded by muffled smirks in the background.

"Yes," I answer nervously.

Even though he's trying to disguise his voice, I can tell it's Steve and a gaggle of his gutless mates and their sisters, my sort-of friends.

"We hate you." Massive laughter and sniggering from the background

"You are a hopeless tennis player. Just give up. You think you are so good, don't you. But you're a big fat loser. Who do you even think you are? No one likes you."

A generation before online bullying becomes a thing, "anonymous" crank calls are the dish of the day.

I lie across the bed sobbing. The shame and humiliation are still seared into my soul today.

I have unconsciously committed social suicide. The message is clear. If you want to stay popular and safe, don't stand out from the crowd. Don't get too big for your boots, Missy. Who am I to challenge the pecking order?

For what won't be the last time in my life I learn that my enthusiasm, eagerness and passion to achieve is mistaken for ego and a desire for attention and that I should reduce myself if I want to fit in. Who do you think you are, Missy?

I learn that people prefer you to be non-threatening. **Containable**.

Until now, I have never told anyone about this incident.

You won't believe this, but just a year or two ago, I clicked on my Facebook account.

A friend request from, yep, Jane Brown. My stomach lurched and my cheeks stung with a memory of 45 years ago. What to do?

I accepted it.

7 — Connection, community & belonging — finding your peeps

"Communication is an exchange of information, but connection is an exchange of our humanity."
— Sean Stephenson

How is it that we are more plugged in thanks to technology and social media than ever before, yet we are more disconnected?

Every MINUTE there are 990,000 Tinder swipes. Yet people are so lonely and isolated?

There's an app and online community for everything. Apparently, we are confronted by more than 10,000 brand advertising messages every day.

Scientists measured the amount of data that confronts our brain each day and found we process information and messages equivalent to watching 16 movies on our computer, mobile phone, TV, tablet and other channels.

There are 500 million tweets posted on Twitter, 100 million images plastered onto Instagram and 4,146,600 videos watched on YouTube every day.

We humans are social animals, a clannish bunch. One look at the groups and labels we give ourselves and others shows how much a sense of belonging matters. We are members of families, sports clubs, teams, online groups, charities, political parties, gender alliances, cities, countries and nationalities ... much of our time is organised around belonging to something.

Yet, despite all these old systems and new ways of digital communication, many of us are lacking meaningful connection. Despite being so connected in some ways, we've never been so cut off from other people and community.

In this era of digital-only relationships, polarised political views and increased disconnection there still seems to be a pervasive sense of being alone — and not in a way where we are renewed by solitude.

Loneliness can be as bad for us as smoking, slicing 15 years off our life expectancy. It has been linked to increased chronic illness and dementia, alcohol abuse, sleep problems, obesity, diabetes, high blood pressure and depression. (14)

The happiest people socialise at least eight hours a day with family, friends, through working and playing. We all need to be part of something.

Even introverts are said to be happier being around people than when they're alone, studies have shown (4).

Writer Brene Brown tells a story about a village where all the women washed clothes together down at the river. When they all got washing machines there was a sudden wave of depression and no one could work out why.

It turns out it wasn't the washing machines; it was the absence of doing things together.

We spend so many hours in front of a computer screen or lost in our phones and are so busy processing info coming from all directions that we are losing the ability to think and feel.

We humans are built to connect. It's why we're here and what gives us purpose and meaning. Why then, is it so hard to fit in?

Hang out with people who fit your future, not your history

The US motivational speaker Jim Rohn reckons we are the average of the five people we hang out with. I'm not sure about the origins of his theory but the gist makes sense. It's a slightly different take on peer pressure.

The people we surround ourselves with have a profound impact on our habits, evolution, happiness and longevity. (It even has a name, the Social Proximity Effect.)

Who we spend our time with has a huge influence on how we behave. Our friends can lead us to bad choices or motivate us to resist them. Statistically, if your three best friends are heavy drinkers or drug takers there's a higher than average chance you'll reflect those characteristics too.

It's the same with attracting the right people into our lives.

Our identity — who we see ourselves as being — is normally based on past beliefs. Most of us decided back when we were kids what we believe, what we are good and bad at, what we can and can't do.

But this can be changed. Our deep-seated beliefs about ourselves can be either a glass ceiling limiting us or a blue sky freeing us. It's not too late to choose.

Unhappy people compare; happy people don't care

A strange thing happens to us when we do start to change, improve and succeed. It can be weirdly threatening and uncomfortable for those around us.

Ever noticed that some friends, family or colleagues seem decidedly unimpressed or displeased for you when success comes your way? They may feel like they are no longer your priority or don't want to lose their connection with you. Or it could be plain old jealousy.

Your good fortune can trigger them to question their own lives. And your success may somehow invalidate their own reasons that they're unhappy or not achieving in the way they may hope.

Or perhaps they don't want to see you grow too far ahead of them. Whatever the underlying cause, don't take it personally; it's all about them.

Even though they may still play an important role in your life, never let an outside voice dampen your spirit or snuff out your light. Surround yourself with people who light and lift you up.

Minister for Loneliness

In the United Kingdom, four in 10 people reported feeling chronic, profound loneliness, which prompted the creation of a Minister for Loneliness to combat the problem.

Japan followed suit in 2022 as mental health problems and suicide rates skyrocketed amid COVID's impact on the nation.

All over the world, the crushing effects of isolation have been compounded by COVID-19 lockdowns.

In Australia, for example, the lockdowns had a significant impact on women's mental health, with 47 per cent — that's nearly one in two — of one study's participants reporting their mental health got worse because of the pandemic. (7)

Top 10 Minute Tips
to help us connect

Making friends doesn't come easily for everyone, so it might require a bit of simple work to improve your people-connecting skills.

1. **It's a health issue**

   People with fewer social connections have higher mortality rates as social isolation can threaten health through lack of access to clinical care, social services or needed support. Loneliness triggers the release of stress hormones associated with higher blood pressure, decreased resistance to infection and increased risk of cardiovascular disease and cancer. There's even evidence that social isolation accelerates cognitive and functional decline and is a preclinical sign for Alzheimer's disease

2. **Your gang. You are who you hang out with**

   Surround yourself with people who lift you up. Remember, your vibe attracts your tribe

3. **Social media**

    Even though social media and the internet can increase feelings of loneliness and cause FOMO (fear of missing out) they can also be a gateway to real support, connection and lasting friendships with people you meet online.

    Naturally, always exercise caution when meeting people via random online platforms. Connect with Facebook or meetup groups focused on your passions. Check to see if any apps you already use, like fitness apps, have a social element or discussion board to join. There are new apps that connect to the neighbourhood where you live or visit

4. **Unfollow toxic people**

    Take 10 minutes to go through your social media accounts and unfollow any whose content makes you feel bad about yourself or less confident. Social media can be toxic, and making this small change will have a huge impact on your mood and stress once you no longer have to see that negative material

5. **Furry friends**

    They can be our best friends and show undying loyalty. Spending time petting a dog can improve your mood and even strengthen your heart. Heart attack patients with pets survive longer than those without. Male pet owners have less sign of heart disease (lower triglyceride and cholesterol levels) than non-owners. Studies have also shown that Alzheimer's patients have fewer anxious outbursts if there is an animal in the home

6.   Crank up your LinkedIn

In 10 minutes you can get some serious mileage out of your LinkedIn account. Update your profile with new skills or achievements, share an interesting link that your connections would enjoy, or join new groups that will help you stay in touch and up to date with industry peers

7.   Hug it out

A hug can make you feel good all day. Sometimes when you don't know what to say, a hug says enough

8.   Buy some time

Take 10 minutes and cancel something on your busy schedule. It will be hard to say no to something at first, but you will feel so relieved after you do it.

Put your hand on it: The power of touch

Touch is really the first language we speak. It kicks in way before sight and speech.

A pat on the back, a hug, one arm linked with the other, a caress … these everyday incidental gestures can improve our health, our mindset, our sense of self and connection. It doesn't take much from the one who gives it, but can make a huge difference to the one who receives it.

Social touch starvation during COVID-19 reinforced what many of us have always known — human touch is profound and fundamental to our health. It is as important as food and can heal, communicate, influence, connect and soothe.

When we hug or feel a friendly touch on our skin, our brains release oxytocin, which increases positive feelings of trust, bonding and social connection while decreasing fear and anxiety. Touch helps regulate our digestion and sleep, and even boosts our immune systems.

Of course, it's essential to have strong boundaries around the appropriate use of touch and to always respect people's personal space.

If touch is absent from your life, and your budget allows, explore healing touch therapies like massage, reiki and acupuncture. Or learn some simple massage and acupressure techniques and take a turn of 10 minutes each with loved ones or friends.

Top 10 Minute Tips to find your peeps

1. Quality over quantity

Gravitate to the right people. Each additional happy friend we have in our social circle boosts our cheeriness by nine per cent, according to one analysis

2. Help out

Volunteering for a cause you believe in brings the benefits of altruism, can help you find more meaning in life, can get you out of the house and gives you perspective. When feeling better about yourself you increase your bandwidth to deal with other things

3. Strengthen existing relationships

Are there people in your life you could get to know better? Reach out to friends more often. Just one supportive friend or family member can make a difference

4. **Music, dance, sing, fun**

    Join a group or put your favourite mix on, turn up the volume and let it rip! Trust me, it works. Find out where there's some local music and ask an acquaintance if they'd be interested in joining you

5. **Laugh**

    It is neurologically impossible to be anxious at the same time we are laughing. Watch a funny show, read a humorous story, search YouTube for things that make you laugh

6. **Man's best friend**

    Pets offer heaps of benefits, including companionship. They can connect you with other people — walking a dog opens up a community of other dog-walkers. People might let you down, but pets give you unconditional love

7. **Talk to strangers**

    Lighten everyday life by interacting in small ways with acquaintances or strangers you come across. I'll leave it to you to use your intuition and discretion and go for more neighbourly than axe murderer vibes!

8. It's not all about you

Be interested in other people and their issues. Ask and listen about their lives, their families, their hobbies, goals, and visions. How you interact directly with others affects the energy of the relationship

9. Put the phone down

Put the iPhone down when you're waiting in a queue or on public transport. Random incidental chats often lead to funny or thought-provoking responses

10. Try something new

Is there something you've been wanting to try? A higher ed course, an art or craft class, singing or dancing lessons, a home improvement project lingering on your to-do list?

11. Join a club

A book, sporting, meditation or other group exposes you to a group of people who share at least one of your interests

12. Say their name

Using an acquaintance's name when talking to them demonstrates you care and are interested. Research shows people feel validated when the person they're speaking with refers to them by name

13. Create your own tribe

If you can't find your peeps, bring together your own group who share a common interest, like swimming or wading

14. Plan your own event

Organise drinks after work, a catch-up at a sporting event, a walk or other activity. If you have the space, have some friends over for a meal or snack

15. Repair small issues

Issues can arise in any relationship. Rather than allowing them to build, address issues while they're small. This might mean apologising or talking it out

16. Smile

People naturally and unconsciously mirror the body language of the person they're talking to. Smile during a conversation and the other person will normally return the favour

17. Manage stress

Everybody has some social situations they dread. Practise simple stress management techniques, like breathing deeply and slowly, to keep the stress in check through awkward moments

18. Commit to making an effort

Making friends doesn't come with a click of the fingers. It requires intention and requires you to push yourself outside of your comfort zone

19. Take the time

A big part of the problem is our perpetual "busyness". Take your 10 minutes each day to focus on how you're going to bring more of the right people into your life

20. Follow the Golden Rule

Just as our parents and teachers told us, treat others as you want to be treated.

Exercise to help you find your peeps

- Shut out distractions

- Close your eyes

- Do a couple of minutes of deep breathing

- Visualise how you'd like your life to look. Add as much detail as possible. What are you wearing? See yourself looking super-happy. Focus on the people around you. What do they look like? Where are you?

- Notice how this picture may look different to the way it used to

- Breathe deeply and focus on the visual image, adding detail in your mind. Notice how it feels

- Say to yourself: "I am living my best life surrounded by kind, fun, quality, supportive people now." Or come up with your own affirmation.

- Say it, see it, feel it

- Plaster the mantra or message on sticky notes everywhere you're comfortable, i.e., a mirror, a bedside table. (Warning, if there are other people around, this can make you look like a d*ck. If so, do it privately.)

Bite-sized bits

"The need for connection and community is primal, as fundamental as the need for air, water, and food."
— Dean Ornish

"Find people who challenge and inspire you and spend a lot of time with them. It will change your life."
— Amy Poehler

"Be here. Be you. Belong."

"Hugs are the universal medicine."

"We are wired for connection. But the key is that, in any given moment of it, it has to be real."
— Brene Brown

"Alone, we can do so little; together, we can do so much."
— Helen Keller

"If you want to go quickly, go alone. If you want to go far, go together."
— African proverb

"Healing yourself is connected with healing others."
— Yoko Ono

Chapter 8

My ex loved to gamble.

A bit like a fast bowler or pitcher when unleashing a bullet , once he decided to open his shoulders with his wallet his vision was steadfast. It could be waging it all a horse or a business deal or taking a chance on a particular person.

He could only ever see the possibility of winning. Losing wasn't an option.

I'd watch in awe as his boldness and risk-taking would result in some fabulous returns. Incredible experiences, luxurious homes, the high life ... the low life. No risk no reward, the saying goes.

I watched him mesmerised at the roulette wheel. Black or red. Odds or evens? High or low?

Just like life, the poker dealer has a bunch of cards in their hands and you get what you're dealt. The best horse doesn't always win, even when the odds say it should. Sometimes there is no reason, or logic or fairness ... the universe seems to have its own plan.

The racetrack and the roulette wheel are in different worlds, yet there is a kinship of sorts. The mob is bound together by a shared passion for excitement, adrenalin, living large on a public stage and — hopefully — winning. The stakes are high. Big wins. Often bigger losses. No guts, no glory.

Business scions, kings and queens, tradies, property developers, and the occasional scoundrel, are attracted to the smell, the energy, the contest and the feeling that anything is possible.

Irrespective of where you come from, if you can stump up the cash and have the temperament for the wild ride you are welcome at the table.

Seeing all this firsthand in full technicolour — and knowing how at home I am among my own tennis mob — teaches me something. (Other than being more judicious before flinging myself down the aisle!)

Our vibe attracts our tribe, as the saying goes.

We all have a fundamental need to belong somewhere. This particular clan is galvanised by a love of risk taking, camaraderie, competition and a sometimes blind belief in the promise of a slice of heaven if you play your cards right.

Take the Wednesday Ocean Waders. Regardless of our shape, size, age, bank balance, social status or profession, we draw strength and energy from each other to strip down to our swimsuits and step into the freezing ocean.

Perhaps there's no more democratic clan? Stripped bare of the pretence of who we are, what we have and who we know, we get to do something bold that we love that would be almost impossible on our own.

It's a rule I have learnt. Our environment determines our behaviour. It's a law of nature and shapes how we choose to live.

So — choose it wisely.

8 — Environment determines behaviour & green space

"Flying starts from the ground. The more grounded you are, the higher you fly."
— J.R. Rim

You're never alone in nature.

There is a strong connection between nature and healing and the relationship between people, place, environment and community. We have two homes — the earth and our body. So best we try to be kind to both.

As our lives have become more broken as a result of stress and mental health challenges, researchers are investigating new ways of looking to nature to heal us.

Something happens when you dive into a world where clocks don't tick and inboxes don't ping. (14)

It would be wrong to think of exercise only as something to build muscle and ease anxiety.

At least sometimes we should force ourselves out of gyms and off machines and into the natural world, knowing that we will come across the salve for our worries.

Research is increasingly showing how these spaces make us feel better physically and mentally. You probably already know and feel it without understanding why. Any keen gardener will tell you about the soothing, sometimes meditative benefits of having your hands in the earth.

Changes to our personal environment nudge us to move more, socialise more and eat better. (4) From the kitchen to our bedroom, to the backyard and into our community.

Sometimes it's as simple as keeping our mouths shut, opening our eyes and just listening.

Making direct contact with the earth allows us to access its energy and healing properties. It might sound woo hoo, but it is scientifically proven. Being in nature lands you back into your body and out of your head, so you can reset and become present.

The call to quiet, to listen and to respect the world we live in is ancient and fundamental. The importance of a connection to country has been known by Indigenous Australians forever. [14]

I've worked in communications in the public health system, where several senior medical staff have told me about the correlation between environment and healing.

Health outcomes of people whose hospital beds have a view of natural light and green spaces are considerably better than those who have no view or who look out onto a brick wall. Patients ask for fewer painkillers and buzz for nurses less often.

When we are exposed to sunlight, trees, water or even just a view of green leaves we become happier, healthier and stronger. People living in green spaces have more energy and a stronger sense of purpose.

Being able to see green spaces from your home is associated with reduced cravings for alcohol, cigarettes and harmful foods. [14]

Numerous studies show the positive effects of daylight on human psychology and health. Access to nature and green environments improves cognitive function;

self-discipline and impulse control; and overall mental health. Less access to nature is linked to attention deficit issues, higher rates of anxiety disorders and depression.

British researchers who looked at data involving more than 290 million people found time spent in green spaces reduces the risk of type 2 diabetes, heart disease, premature death, preterm birth and stress, and improves mental health and blood pressure.

We instinctively gravitate to environments that are comfortable and familiar. Gambling, hospitality, and retail experts know this well and deliver an atmosphere that offers comfort and entertainment with a feeling of safety.

Nothing in casinos or stores happens by accident. Even if it might seem like you have free will to roam, clever shop and casino design dictates where most shoppers and gamblers will go and predicts their behaviour patterns.

Control the controllables

Chaos can drive us crazy, and order restores balance. Sort out your computer files, your kitchen cupboards, your underwear drawer.

Grounding

Barefoot healing, known as earthing or grounding, is said to offer several health benefits and — despite being around for hundreds of years — is in vogue right now.

We don't get a chance to touch the earth directly in our modern day-to-day lives like we used to. Instead, we're exposed to things like television, mobile phones and computers.

Shoes, buildings and cars all insulate us from the earth's surface. Without this connection to the earth, supporters of this practice tell us, our bodies aren't drawing in the "negative charge to balance the positive charge" which helps harmonise our bodies.

Earthing is the therapeutic practice of physically connecting your body to the surface of the earth. Proponents report less inflammation and physical disease and improved mental health

10 Minute grounding exercise

- Remove your shoes and walk with bare feet on dirt, grass or sand

- Sit or lie directly on the earth, without being insulated by anything such as wood, plastic or rubber in the form of, say, furniture or a yoga mat

- Place your hands into soil to feel grounded

Benefits can include

- Improve sleep

- Reduce inflammation

- Improve overall health

- Relieve headaches

- Assist with chronic pain

- Improve mental health.

Tips to connect with Mother Nature

- Work on your laptop in the park

- Catch up with friends, colleagues or family in the fresh air of a park or beach instead of a bar or cafe

- Have a walking meeting instead of gathering in a stuffy boardroom or office

- Meditate outside

- Open your windows daily to release the stale air

- Get some indoor plants. NASA has researched how plants provide clean air.

Tips on being kind to the earth

- Turn off the tap while you brush your teeth

- Switch to paperless billing

- Recycle. Look for treasures in opportunity shops or online and always donate your clothes and furniture when it's time to part with them

- Use energy-efficient light bulbs

- Use a refillable water bottle

- Take cloth bags to the supermarket

- Reduce packaging by supporting farmers markets. Look for fruit and vegetable home delivery services and try the fresh bulk-food stores

- Swap single-use coffee pods for a coffee plunger or machine

- Carbonate your own fizzy drinks to reduce plastic bottles

- Switch from disposable razors to a safety razor where only the blades need to be replaced.

Did you know?

By 2050 the ocean will contain more plastic than fish if we don't start changing today.

The 5H rule

When buying gifts go for handmade, homemade, healthy, helpful and here (made locally).

Home is a feeling

Our living spaces have a big impact on our mental and physical health.

Your home is where you spend most of your time, so it's important that it's a place where you feel well.

A house doesn't have to be fancy or on-trend to be a beautiful haven. Often the homes that feel the most comfortable are older, smaller and filled with character, charm and warmth.

You may not have a permanent home. Or you may have little control over the space in which you live. You may have a room, a share arrangement, a swag or something more fleeting.

Wherever you lay your hat or heart, the trick is to surround yourself with things, colours, spaces and people you love. Home isn't necessarily a place, it's a feeling.

Declutter, discard, donate, ditch ... oh, the agony!

If our wardrobe is a metaphor for our life, I'm f*cked.

This is a case of do as I say, not what I do!

But I do know that the first step in crafting the life you want is to get rid of everything you don't.

Japanese professional junk clearer Marie Kondo reckons if something isn't giving you joy, ditch it. She says that tidying and clearing can be life-changing, and creating space in our lives means we attract new things. Clutter blocks energy flow. I know. I know.

I have been accused of low-level hoarding. But I am a *collector*. A lover of fine, well, things. Stuff.

But my things are not merely things. They contain messages, memories or feelings I want to keep or relive.

Psychologists say true hoarding — and I'm not making light of it — is a painful and sometimes crippling disorder requiring understanding and professional support. It can reflect procrastination, indecisiveness, perfectionism and disorganisation.

However, using the small-steps 10 Minute principle, moving stuck energy from our home, mind and heart can create a beautiful ripple effect of change. There is a link between clearing physical and emotional clutter and calming the sense of being overwhelmed.

I'm told that ditching some of my stuff will give me a new sense of clarity and a greater feeling of ease.

So, as I type this, I am taking 10-minute breaks to delve into my bulging drawers and wardrobe and ask myself: "What am I holding onto that no longer makes sense?"

Top 10 Minute clearing tips to change your Life

· ·

1. **Starting small is easier**

Pick one thing and get started. Declutter one spot. Thinking about sorting the whole house can be overwhelming

- ◆ The process gets easier as you create natural momentum and gain more and more energy with each cleared space

2. **Make your bed**

If you make your bed every morning, you will have accomplished the first task of the day. It will give you a small sense of pride and encourage you to do another task. And another. By the end of the day that one task completed may have turned into many small achievements.

3. **Email clutter**

- ◆ Unsubscribe from email lists

- ◆ Clear out your inbox and junk

4. **Yum — it'll taste better**
  - In your kitchen:
  - Have the healthiest ingredients on hand
  - Create a no-devices zone
  - Play music that moves you

5. **Let's talk about sex, baby**
  In your bedroom:
  - An undistracting bedroom is more conducive to better sexual energy. (That's what they tell me anyway!)

6. **Sleep, come free me**
  In your bedroom:
  - Invest in a comfortable mattress and pillows
  - Dim the lights about an hour before bed
  - Remove computers, phones, TV screens and digital alarm clocks. If there's a TV, unplug it so the little red lights are off
  - Block the outside light with blinds

7, **Control the controllables**
  - Organise your desktop
  - Clean out your wallet, handbag or backpack
  - Clean out a junk drawer

8.   Home is where the heart is

- Clear your benchtops

- Recycle or shred old papers

- Clear out the fridge

- Clean out the junk drawer

- Sweep, vacuum, mop

9.   Toss the toiletries

- Before brushing your teeth or jumping in the shower in the morning, if you're not in a hurry spend 10 minutes getting rid of old, half-used and unwanted toiletries.

10.   The 10 Things dash

- Walk into each room of your home with a box or garbage bag. Then choose 10 things you can throw out or donate. Choose duplicates or items that are worn out, outdated or rarely used.

Do the season-swapsy

- Stow away last season's stuff. Be sure to wash or dry-clean clothes before storing, even if they look clean. If you don't have an extra cupboard, try vacuum packing.

Bite-sized bits

"Look deep into nature and then you
will understand everything better."
— Albert Einstein

"Choose only one master — nature."
— Rembrandt

"One of the first conditions of happiness is that the link
between man and nature must not be broken."
— Leo Tolstoy

"Of all the paths you take in life,
make sure a few of them are dirt."

"We shape our buildings and afterwards
our buildings shape us."
— Winston Churchill

"The one who remained grounded is the
one who reached heights."
— AnShii

"Have nothing in your house that you do not
know to be useful or believe to be beautiful."
— William Morris

"The question of what you want to own is
actually the question of how you want to live your life."
— Marie Kondo

"Minimalism isn't about removing things you love. It's
about removing the things that distract you from the
things you love."
— Joshua Becker

Chapter 9

I am living in a time before the universe decided that everyone deserves a participation award or should be rewarded with interesting activities that they might actually enjoy.

Playground teams are chosen by two self-appointed captains. They choose the best athletes, picking them off one by one until the kids who are the most hopeless at sport or really small or — God forbid — disabled, stand there looking like complete losers.

I'm a big girl now — grade four. It's a small, unremarkable Catholic primary school in the suburbs where there's no time for blowing sunshine or getting ahead of yourself.

I am sitting in the drab classroom with Carla, notable in our playground for being a glamourous child model who featured on a washing powder box. It's just the two of us.

We are supposed to be writing in our exercise books while our teacher, Sister Marie, attends to much more important duties elsewhere: school choir practice. But our books are sitting there empty as we both feel pretty stupid.

Just a week earlier I remember being so anxious and nervous. Every student from grades four, five and six had to audition and sing a few lines of some dreary dirge on their own. In front of the no-fuss nun who sat in judgment.

Every single student except for Carla and myself was accepted into the choir. (BTW I'm sure I had a cold that day, but no doubt that's just hubris!)

"Oh, you really do not have a good voice," Sister Marie tells me. "You cannot sing."

I presume she delivers the same delicate appraisal to my fellow songbird Carla.

"Don't you wish we were with the other kids?" I ask Carla. I know there is nowhere in the whole world I'd rather be. At that moment I would do anything not to be an outcast and to be part of the group. Even if that means a dumb choir singing a boring hymn.

"Nah," she says defiantly. I'm impressed. *"I wouldn't want to be with those losers."*

"Me neither," I lie.

All these years later I still cannot sing. And I can't speak for Carla, but I am fairly confident that my choral silencing hasn't been a significant loss to the world of music.

But there is no doubt that the harsh assessment of my abilities crushed any thoughts I might have had of enjoying crooning outside of my shower.

I have since discovered that while some people are born with a natural gift, for the rest of us mortals the art or act of singing can be taught. It's a learned skill, but not one I have ever been brave enough to expose myself to again.

I have, however, dedicated much of my professional life to heeding the lesson I learnt that day. What We Say Matters.

Words have the power to humiliate, hurt, harm, hinder — and to heal.

So, I became a writer.

9 — Words & affirmations

"When words are both true and kind,
they can change the world."
— Buddha

Words have power.

So, like your friends, choose them wisely.

Words can be horrible or helpful. You choose.

The good news about words is they can transform our lives. The bad news is, if we are not careful, it can be for the worse.

Whether spoken, written, or just the words we use in our own minds, handle them carefully as they have more power than atom bombs.

Words are more than just a way to communicate, because they have "energy", a vibration and power that generates emotional responses when we read, speak or hear them. They shape how we view the world.

Sound a bit woohoo? Don't believe me? Consider what would happen if you walked into a packed movie theatre and yelled out one little word: FIRE!

There would be responses ranging from panic and disbelief to fear, anger, confusion, calm or composure depending on whatever emotional connection and personal history those four simple little letters triggered.

Or spend a few minutes with a chronic complainer who whinges about everything and then watch how, if you're not careful, your personal energy is sapped. Negative energy has a way of dragging everything surrounding it in, like a big black hole. Avoid it.

Words are free. It's how you use them that may cost you

Are you talking about possibilities or problems?

Using positive words that inspire you every day will change your thoughts, energy, actions and most importantly, results. Even the science says this attracts more positive energy to you. Your odds of success are so much better.

Using negative words, or self-defeating language attracts more negative circumstances and pushes you further away from what you want.

This is one reason that journaling and affirmations can work.

It's only after being burned a few times that we understand fire is always hot. Repetition is the most powerful tool to imprint something on our minds.

Often we use the same negative words over and over out of habit. The problem is that the more we hear, read or speak a word or phrase, the more power it has over us. The brain uses repetition to learn.

This is one of the reasons — regardless of your take on religion or spirituality — chanting and prayer can be so powerful.

Did you know?

The average person has 12,000 to 60,000 thoughts a day?

We are constantly talking to ourselves. That's a lot of words spinning around in our heads. Make them work for you, not against you.

Exercise

Don't believe words can influence behaviour? Try this exercise

◆ Close your eyes and imagine a big, juicy lemon

◆ Hold it, feel the texture, smell that unique citrus aroma

◆ Picture cutting the lemon with a sharp knife and notice the juice dripping down its side

◆ Cut again into quarters and put a piece in your mouth. Take a nice juicy bite

◆ Note the experience in your mouth

◆ Yep, your mouth has started to water and produce extra saliva. Told ya.

So how does this even work? Apparently, the mind can't distinguish between real and imagined events. You can either imagine eating the lemon or really eat the lemon and your brain will consider it the same.

I will say affirmations. Repeat.
I WILL say affirmations

Countless studies have proven the healing effect that saying positive affirmations can have on our overall wellbeing — regardless of how uncomfortable it feels to tell ourselves how amazing we are.

An affirmation is usually a sentence of powerful, positive, purposeful words which we use to tap into our conscious and unconscious minds to motivate, challenge and push us to reach our goals.

It's normal to have negative and unhelpful thoughts, but affirmations when spoken, written or chanted to ourselves have the power to change the way we think and act. There is a wealth of research and anecdotal evidence that shows affirmations — if repeated several times a day for at least 10 minutes — can lead to positive change.

For affirmations to work, you need to believe what you are saying. The richer, bigger, more colourful, three-dimensional and clear, the better.

For example: *"All I need for success is already within me."* You need to believe the statement and repeat it at least three to five times a day for it to weave any magic.

Careful what you wish for

When we use our creative energy, unconsciously we can create what is commonly known as a self-fulfilling prophecy. When we worry, we repeatedly focus our energy on creating something we don't want. But we can retrain our minds and thoughts to focus our energy on what we do want to bring into our lives.

The simplest antidote to worry is affirmations. When we hold these positive thoughts, repeat them often, speak them and write them and refer to them throughout our day, we are using focused energy to create positive results.

Did you know?

Saying where's the butter, where's the butter, where's the butter means you're more likely to find it? True story.

Practise affirmations

1. Start with three to five minutes at least twice a day. Say a couple of key affirmations when you wake up and get into bed, for example

2. Ensure they are positive and in the present

3. Say it, see it, believe it

4. Repeat each affirmation.

Here are a few easy options to start:

- I am at peace now and surrounded by love

- I am creating my own happiness

- My challenges are actually opportunities

- I am strong, healthy and beautiful just the way I am

- I get better and better every day

- All I need is within me right now

- I am an unstoppable force of nature

- I respect my boundaries and stand in my power

- I am grateful and give thanks for what I have

- The more I give, the more I receive. The more I receive, the more I give

- I allow my life to flow

- I love and accept myself just as I am

- I am enough. I am worthy

- I attract fabulous people into my life

- I release and let go of anything that doesn't serve my higher purpose

- I am energised and attract prosperity and abundance into my life.

Disclaimer: It's OK to feel real. Sometimes life sucks

Telling ourselves that we are eating lobster when we are actually eating tinned tuna will not make it so.

Just because you want to feel a certain way, doesn't make the other feelings go away. They are still there needing to be dealt with.

Despite all the evidence about the importance of positive self-talk and creating change, sometimes negativity is just the way it is. Shiz happens.

Relationships break up, people get sick, jobs flop, loved ones pass, people get depressed, we screw up, anxiety kicks in. And it's stupid to pretend that it's not happening and immediately put a positive spin on it.

We need to allow ourselves the grace to feel all our emotions, whether they are positive or negative.

When the time is right, pick yourself up and get (re) started. Just 10 minutes can help.

Words at work: journaling

Journaling can be the most cost-effective therapy you'll find.

Studies show that using a pen and journal is the best way to bypass the thinking mind, move mental blocks and tap into your intuition. Getting everything out of your head and onto the page not only feels like a relief and brings clarity, it can also sometimes stop you from saying hurtful things you might regret.

It helps track habits and patterns and is a gateway for creative ideas and solutions.

Tips

How to start journaling

1. Find a journal or notebook that you like or that inspires you

2. Decide what type of journaling you'd like to try and just start. There is no wrong way to journal

3. Take 10 minutes to write about something positive that happened in the previous 24 hours.

Top 10 Minute Tips

1. **Change your passwords**. I recently read about a guy who used this specific password technique to process his anger after his divorce. He changed his password to Forgive@h3r, and it worked. His next password was Quit@smoking4ever, and it helped him quit smoking. Think about how many times you enter a password during your day. Make it something that is going to help you create the environment you want

2. **Do a brain dump**. Counterproductive thoughts and emotions build up. The anger you feel towards a friend, anxiety about missing an important work deadline or frustration from being turned down for a promotion all need to be processed. Your worst-case-scenario thinking won't improve until you get it all out of your head. It's amazing how different a problem looks when it's on paper

3. **"If ... then" a goal**. Research has shown that if you add "if ... then" statements to your goals, the likelihood of achieving those goals increases. For example, use "if ... then" statements with your health goals: "If it's

Monday morning, then I'm going to the gym." That becomes a habit, which puts your brain on autopilot. If it's cold outside, you're tired or you just don't feel like going, it doesn't matter, because it's Monday morning, and Monday morning = the gym

4. **Your words at work.** Everyone is doing the best they can with the info they have, including you. Be kind and offer yourself the same empathy and compassion you'd extend to anyone else. Resist gossiping and speaking poorly of others

5. **Go on a negativity diet.** Instead of saying that a meal was terrible, try saying, "I've had better." You've still said what you wanted without tapping into negative energy — you've even used a positive word to do it!

6. **Nix the negative Nancys.** If you have some negative types in your circle of friends, limit the time you spend with them or share activity-based time, limiting the convo time

7. **Surround yourself with positive, uplifting words.** Put affirmations on sticky notes around your home and office that say fab things about you, your family or your goals. As you keep doing it you use the power of repetition for your benefit. You have the power to change your world, and using words consciously is one of the quickest ways to shift the energy.

Bite-sized bits

"Be careful what you say. You can say something
hurtful in 10 seconds, but 10 years later,
the wounds are still there."
— Osteen

"What you think, you become."
– Buddha

"Words are free. It's how you use them
that may cost you."
— Kushand Wizdom

"Raise your words, not your voice.
It is rain that grows flowers, not thunder."
– Rumi

"All I need is a sheet of paper and something to write
with, and then I can turn the world upside down."
– Friedrich Nietzsche

"Your words have power. Speak words that are kind,
loving, positive, uplifting, encouraging, and life-giving."

"Words and ideas can change the world."
– John Keating

"Whether you think you can,
or you think you can't, you're right."
– Henry Ford

Chapter 10

It should be a day of pride and satisfaction.

Instead, I'm feeling out of sorts. I wear the slightly ludicrous cap and gown and accept my bachelor's degree in front of a very proud mum, Effie — who had the immense pleasure of seeing all five of her children graduate — and my sister Pamela. We had trudged off in our best clothes out to the suburban campus for the ceremony.

Afterwards, we go to the house of my sister Michelle and her husband, Glenn, for a family celebration. My other sister, Denise, and my brother, John, gather around the table as candles are poked into the baby blue icing of one of Mum's famous and delicious four-egg sponges. They all sing comically, "Happy Graduation to you, Happy Graduation to youuuuuuu."

I joylessly blow out the candles. I have my piece of cake. Then another.

It's supposed to be a jubilant moment. But the walls start to close in.

Up until now I have always been small and slim. Playing so much tennis and lots of other sport means I have got into some bad food habits as I'm accustomed to eating large amounts of whatever I want and burning it off. And never putting on weight.

But I have discovered boys and alcohol and life, which has cruelled my aspiring tennis career! With the same enthusiasm and commitment, I have replaced sport with cigarettes and dancing on tables. It's party town.

A late developer, I seem to have new fleshy bits in strange places of my body. Where did these come from? My bosoms are huge and, frankly, I don't know where to put them. They look ludicrous bursting out of the tidy little singlets and tops I've always favoured.

Things are getting weird with my boyfriend of six years — we'll call him Markie. While the rest of my gang are playing the field, I like the stability that the constancy a loving male brings. (Yep, a shrink would rightly identify daddy issues coming to the fore!)

Except nothing is stable about Markie.

It's a tragedy and a far deeper story. But in brief, where others we know may be able to flirt with drugs and alcohol in the name of fun, he seems to have a far different relationship with the poison.

There are a lot of lies, erratic behaviour, tearful apologies and promises of redemption. None of it can mask the gut-wrenching reality that dear, sweet, handsome Markie is now a heroin addict.

I sit gloomily in my sister's loungeroom. I have another piece of cake.

The chatter in the room starts to whir in my head. I feel out of control and fearful for the future. I look at my body with disgust. I feel fat and I hate myself.

I slip out to the bathroom. I kneel on the floor in front of the toilet. I pull my hair back, lean my face over the bowl and plunge two fingers deep down my throat.

There's a gagging response. It's a bit hard at first and not much happens. But I stick with it and soon a noxious waterfall of mushed-up, delicate egg sponge and tea and lemonade comes gushing out and lands in the bowl.

I am ashamed of what I have done. My day of supposed triumph has turned toxic. But part of me feels empowered as I think I have cracked the code of what women all over the world have been trying to discover.

I think I have found a way to eat whatever I want and still be in control of my weight.

10 — Nourishment & weight management

"Let food be your medicine and medicine be your food."

The way we eat is the most basic way we show care for ourselves.

But for some it can be complex, marked by distress and despair. And if this is the case for you, know you aren't alone and there's help at hand. Please consult a trained professional.

One thing I know for sure is that no long-term change ever comes from deprivation. It comes from kindness. And there's an intimate connection between what we eat and how we feel.

Consuming nourishing food is the basis for exceptional health.

While there's no "one size fits all", how you nourish your body is your best barometer. Notice how certain foods make you feel and identify any patterns.

For me, it was important to stop viewing food as the enemy and see it as the source of my vitality and energy, and something incredibly enjoyable. I needed to try to shift the focus from how my body looked to what it could do, where it could take me and how amazing it could feel.

After I worked through underlying issues and created a balanced pattern of nourishment, exercise, rest, mindfulness, a positive body image and eating with family, friends and a sense of fun, my body weight now mostly regulates itself.

My personal philosophy is: stop dieting and start nourishing. I eat with pleasure, appreciation and thanks. Count blessings and nutrients rather than calories. What I eat and drink has a powerful effect on my ability to focus, mental clarity, mood, stress and energy levels.

But I know we are all different. I am not an expert in diet or psychology, so my advice is simple. Be gentle and kind on yourself. If you want change or need help, reach for it in an appropriate, sensible and supported place.

Real food, according to *New York Times* best-selling food author Michael Pollan, is something you haven't seen an ad for. The less packaged the better.

But even healthy eating can be, well, unhealthy, if you listen to him. Apart from the well-documented poor American diet, people are now developing a negative obsession with healthy eating too, he says. So, let's just chill a little …

"The American paradox is we are a people who worry unreasonably about dietary health yet have the worst diet in the world," he writes.

The average American adult consumes 36 kilograms of fat and 8000 teaspoons of added sugar annually, washed down with 216 litres of soft drink. (4)

It's even worse in Canada, with the average person consuming 26 teaspoons of sugar each day or 9500 each year.

Overall, Australians consume more than 2.4 billion litres of sugary drinks every year. That's enough to fill 960 Olympic swimming pools. We swallow an average of 60 grams, or 14 teaspoons, of white sugar each day, mostly coming from "treats" and drinks.

The World Health Organisation suggests less than 25 grams, or six teaspoons, a day ideally.

An Australian Bureau of Statistics study found that 67 per cent of Australian adults — 12.5 million people — are overweight or obese.

And in the UK, more than 42 million adults, or 71 per cent, will be overweight or obese by 2040 and at higher risk of 13 types of cancer, according to a 2022 study.

Poor understanding of food and food choices, together with a lack of understanding of the connection between what we eat and our emotions, are fuelling the Western world's increasing obesity crisis and a range of other health problems.

Most experts agree restrictive diets are largely a useless strategy to lose and maintain weight. To achieve your desired weight, equip yourself with the facts of nutrition, quit the diets, eat fresh and focus on self-love (or at least settle for self-*like*), not self-loathing.

And if that's still not working for you, seek support from a respected source.

Disordered eating is complex and has profound and sometimes devastating emotional and physical effects. There are trained experts who understand the complexities and how to help people dealing with the problem. There is no shame in asking for help. Please, please, please seek help if you're struggling. You are not alone.

The link between food & mood

Get "hangry" when dinner is late? Clouded by brain fog at 3pm? If you find yourself reaching for the biscuit tin mid-afternoon, you're not the only one. Many of us find ourselves trying to boost our mood with a sugar hit.

Unfortunately, while it might feel like a good short-term fix, it can make a low mood worse.

Food has a big impact on our mood changes and mental wellbeing. But what foods should we be eating to support better mental health?

Food fuels mind and body. We eat nutritious foods so our bodies grow, repair and function well. Our brain needs nutritious foods too. In fact, it's quite hungry — the brain accounts for 20 per cent of our total daily energy requirements.

Choosing nutritious foods provides our body and brain with the building blocks needed to be at our best. From vitamins and minerals to healthy fats and fibre, nutrients play a role in brain health and function.

Healthy eating is linked to better stress management, sleep quality, concentration, and mental wellbeing. Just as our food choices affect our mental wellbeing, the opposite is also true — we're more likely to follow a healthy diet when we're in a good headspace. (15)

Did you know?

Of the 100 people who start a diet today, fewer than five per cent will still be on that diet maintenance plan two years later (4)

10 Tips to improve our relationship with food & body image

1. **Listen to your body.** Eat when you are hungry and rest when you are tired

2. **Change the messages you give yourself.** Identify the negative ways that you speak to yourself and decide to replace them with more realistic, kind and positive statements

3. **Throw out the bathroom scales.** You are much more than a number on a scale. Instead focus on the most important things about yourself, like your unique talents, qualities and skills

4. **Think of your body as an instrument instead of as an ornament.** Be thankful every day for the fab things you can do in your body, such as dance, make love, play, run, enjoy good food and give hugs

5. **Exercise to feel good and be healthy**, not to lose weight or punish your body. Find fun ways to add more physical activity in your life, such as walking with a friend

6. **Move with your head held high.** If you act like someone with a healthy body image and good self-confidence, the "act" will eventually become reality

7. **Wear comfortable clothes that fit.** Clothes that are too big or too small tend to create physical discomfort and may make you feel worse about your body. Clothes that are comfortable and fit well are designed to complement your figure. Ignore size tags if possible, because you are not a number

8. **Question ads that perpetuate unrealistic standards for our bodies.** Instead of saying, "What's wrong with me?" say, "What's wrong with this ad?" Set your own standards

9. **Surround yourself with people who are supportive of you and your bod.** If your partner or friends are critical of your body, it's time to re-evaluate the relationship

Every day tell yourself: "My body is amazing and does very cool things!" Exposing your most intimate and complex relationship — the one with yourself — is confronting. I wasn't even sure I was allowed to love my body as I thought it was kind of being up yourself. Who cares!

Mito-what? Why are mitochondria important?

Nutrients, which we turn into energy, fuel our body's cells, which have tiny generators called mitochondria. Optimising our mitochondria can improve overall health by:

- Increasing energy levels

- Slowing cellular ageing

- Increasing support for our organs

- Boosting physical performance and reducing recovery times

- Promoting better sleep

- Aiding clarity and mental focus

- Leading to visibly healthier skin.

Top 10 ways to boost our mitochondria

1. **Eat fewer calories.** Calorie reduction lowers production of free radicals and improves mitochondrial function

2. **Eat two to three meals within an eight to 10-hour window.** Intermittent fasting removes damaged mitochondria and triggers new mitochondria. A meal-timing schedule that mimics our natural circadian rhythm is to eat three meals a day, at 8am, 12pm and 5pm

3. **Throw away refined carbs like soda, white bread and pastries**

4. **Eat quality protein like grass-fed beef and pasture-raised eggs**

5. **Eat sources of omega-3s and alpha-lipoic acid.** Add wild-caught salmon, halibut, sardines and anchovies. Combine with vegetables such as spinach, broccoli, yams, brussels sprouts, carrots or beets as sources of alpha-lipoic acid

6. **Eat antioxidant-rich foods.** Grapes, red wine, dark chocolate and pistachios are beneficial if ingested in moderation

7. **Daily physical activity.** Physical exercise is the best way to increase our oxygen intake, which is critical for mitochondria

8. **Try heat therapy.** Aim for two or three sauna sessions a week for at least 10 minutes

9. **Reduce stress with relaxation techniques.** Stress hormones can alter mitochondrial function, which affects biological processes, especially the immune, nervous and endocrine systems. Create a stress reduction routine with just a few minutes of guided meditation daily. **(See Chapter 6)**

10. **Prioritise eight hours of sleep a night.** Sleep allows our brain to clear the neural waste.

Booze

I really like drinking alcohol. But our relationship is unrequited because alcohol really doesn't like me. It robs me of clarity and purpose, and it takes the edge off my vitality. But it can be so much fun! We are all different, so get real with yourself about how alcohol affects you. And make choices that work for you.

Alcohol tips

- Even if you're happy being an enthusiastic drinker, schedule in a few alcohol-free days each week

- Before you dive in, have a big glass of water to see if it reduces your desire for alcohol

- Have a healthy snack before you have a drink to cut the unending desire for salty chips

- Be sociable. Residents of the world's longest-living zones have a glass of wine at 5pm every day with friends **(See Chapter 12)**. Do they get drunk? Nope. When they drink, do they engage with people who matter to them? Yep.

Learn to love what you eat

Focus on what your body can do, not what it looks like.

Throw out the calories-in versus calories-out mindset and focus on nourishment. I learned that if I throw together a salad full of veggies, nuts, seeds, avocado, protein and homemade dressing, I won't keep demanding food all afternoon.

Eat with complete attention

Put away your screens. Savour your meal, noticing all its tastes and textures. You'll improve your digestion, feel more relaxed and improve your relationship with food.

The four best foods to have on hand

- **Nuts:** Handful a day

- **Beans:** Either dry or canned

- **Good bread:** Wholegrain from a local artisan baker for sandwiches or toast. Try sprouted grain. If you can squeeze a slice of bread into a ball, avoid it

- **Fruit and vegetables**: Fresh and locally grown.

The four foods to avoid

Sugar-sweetened drinks: Empty calories and bad for brain health

Salty snacks like potato chips: It's a shame because they taste good, but they have too much salt and preservatives

Processed meat: Linked to cancer and heart disease

Packaged lollies and sweets: Biscuits, cookies, lollies ... the sugar hit spikes blood sugar and is not great for the brain.

Top 10 Minute Tips
to change your life

- Throw out anything with the word "diet" or "modified"

- Eat whole and unprocessed foods

- Use olive oil instead of butter. Drizzle onto vegetables, salads and wholegrain bread

- Stock up on whole grains like oats, barley, brown rice and ground corn

- Use leftover veggies to make vegetable soup or freeze for later

- Reduce meat intake

- Eat with friends and family. "Breaking bread" together is galvanising

- Eat mindfully

- Never eat standing up

- Never eat while driving

- Never eat while working

- Cut out sugar, make honey your go-to sweetener

- A piece of fruit can be your sweet treat

- Watch out for processed foods and condiments — particularly, salad dressing and tomato sauce

- Avoid low-fat products. Some — like low-fat yoghurt — contain more sugar per ounce than soft drinks

- Eat some nuts before a meal to reduce the overall glycaemic load

- Learn to love your body no matter what. (I know that's a pretty loaded sentence! But give it a crack.)

Bite-sized bits

"Food brings people together on many different levels. It's
nourishment of the soul and body."
— Giada De Laurentiis

"We all eat, and it would be a sad waste
of opportunity to eat badly."

"You don't need a silver fork to eat good food."

"Laugher is brightest where food is best."
— Irish proverb

"If more of us valued food and cheer and song above
hoarded gold it would be a merrier world."
— J.R.R. Tolkien

"I only drink champagne on two occasions, when I am in
love and when I am not."
— Coco Chanel

"Food is essential to life, therefore, make it good."

"Food is culture and identity."

"After a good dinner, one can forgive anybody,
even one's own relations."
— Oscar Wilde

Chapter 11

It's not a recommended recovery strategy — and it may well set feminism back a thousand years, but the time comes when I start to get a lot of positive attention for my body, which makes me look at myself differently. Oh, more complexity.

Unfortunately, my newfound, perfectly formed, big bazoomers and overall shape have started turning heads.

"Wearing one of those busty tops again, I see," a male colleague observes lustily.

I look down in horror.

I dress so carefully to hide my bosom in this hormone-charged and male-dominated newspaper office where I've just started work as a graduate cadet journalist — and where a running commentary on all the females' form is daily sport.

"It's not the shirt that's the problem; they're my lady bits and there's just nowhere to put them," I want to yell. Instead, I demur politely.

I hate the unwanted leering, which makes me feel even more self-conscious. It's bad enough that I scrutinise myself so harshly, now the whole world seems to have an opinion on my curves and edges.

While I hate being objectified, a weird thing happens. The feedback is inappropriate, but I find it affirming and it starts to take the edge off my self-loathing.

Underneath my spiritual nature, I am a logical and practical person.

If my body were so horrendous, nobody would mention it. They certainly would not talk about it in such lustful tones. So, it may be time to make peace with my body myself.

I know how perilous it is to judge self-worth on the evaluation of others — particularly in something as shallow as my looks or body shape. But I use the approval of others as permission to approve of myself.

It might be a bit twisted, but I'm struggling so I'll take it. And I start to feel less out of control.

It helps me step out from a delayed adolescence and sometimes haunted past into womanhood and to find some peace with myself.

I break away from two destructive relationships — one with Markie, and one with me.

I learn a concept that, while I don't know it right now, will stay with me for life — even prompting me to write this book.

"For things to change, first I must change."

We waste our energy willing other people to change. "Just stop taking drugs." "Give up the drink". "Stop that destructive habit." "If you change this one thing everything will be perfect."

No matter how simple, obvious and accurate our wishes for other people may be, there is nothing we can actually do about it. Any change — no matter how blindly obvious it is necessary — is purely their choice. You cannot change other people. The only person you have real agency over is yourself.

So, I put my two fingers back in the holster.

No more purging. (Although unhealthy thought patterns will continue to lurch in and out over the years as challenges come and go). I rediscover a love of moving my body. Exercise and sport are really the ultimate acts of change because it's all about motion. Moving the energy.

I realise some people use exercise as punishment for overindulging or shaming themselves to be a certain way. Our relationship with our bodies can be a strange and complex thing.

But despite the awful experience with the two-finger quick draw, exercise is not about that for me.

I thrive when I'm moving. The endorphins kick in, I feel good in myself, I smile, my mind frees, I'm in flow. It's my passion and my happy place.

I now look at my beautiful, unique body with kinder eyes. Through the lens of respect — not disordered thinking.

See ya, self-hate. Hello, self-care.

It's time you get moving again, I say to myself. You've got people to meet and places to go.

So I take up running for fun.

11 — Movement & exercise

"Consciousness is only possible through change; change is only possible through movement."
— **Aldous Huxley**

Seriously? Ten minutes? Surely that's not all it takes?

If you extrapolate it over a full year, that's 60 hours of exercise you may not have been doing otherwise! Ten minutes a day can really add up to something significant.

There are just not enough hours in the day to do it all — love, move, nourish, be in nature, get enough sleep, mindfulness, gratitude. Don't forget you have to write in your journal and say your affirmations! Oh, and then there's work or school or family or fun.

But 10 minutes a day feels like it's doable, even on the days when you really don't want to do it.

So how can you put your mental and physical health first every day and still do the other things on your list? The answer is to integrate small rituals or habits into each day.

It's the classic, if you don't put your own oxygen mask on first you can't help others. Just 10 minutes walking around the block can improve your mood, mental and physical health — and motivation to get moving to do other things.

The key is to establish the foundation for a daily practice.

Ten-minute exercise bites are not necessarily your fitness end goal. But they are enough to get you out of bed and get you moving. To make you feel like you did something when you're done, shift your energy when you're stuck or don't have time for more.

Some exercise physiologists and researchers are calling these bite-sized bursts "exercise snacks" or "micro-workouts".

Ten-minute workouts are better than not exercising at all. They can also assist you to establish an exercise routine, which is particularly helpful if you're not currently active.

And, of course, who says you have to stop at 10 minutes.

Did you know/

10 minutes of exercise has been proven to:

- Stabilise blood sugar levels

- Improve cognitive focus and mood

- Improve cardiovascular fitness

- Increase your motivation

- Save you time.

Did you know/

If adults aged 40 to 85 engaged in just 10 additional minutes of moderate to vigorous physical activity a day, it would save 110,000 deaths a year.

(source: Journal of the American Medical Association Internal Medicine)

Exercise snacks

- There is overwhelming evidence that even a 10-minute workout performed at moderate to high intensity can make a huge difference to your health and your fitness level

- Studies show that short, intense workouts help boost calorie burning long after you're finished working out

- Exercise is more important as a person gets older because it can slow down the effects of ageing

- Pick a type of exercise that best fits your schedule

- You can also start with a small amount and build that up over time.

Regular exercise benefits virtually every organ system in our body. It reduces blood pressure, blood sugar and cholesterol levels. Exercise can also help us sleep better and improve our mood and quality of life.

Healthy relationship with your body

- Avoid self-talk that reinforces a problematic relationship between exercise and food. Mentally separate food from exercise

- Learn to listen to your body. Our bodies have a natural desire to move

- Focus on gains from exercise other than weight loss

- Enjoy yourself!

10-minute exercise session

- Walk up and down the stairs 10 times

- Place your hands on a step and do 10 push-ups

- Do 10-20 jumping jacks

- Place your hands on the lower stair, on a stable chair or couch and hold in plank position for a count to 30.

10 Minute workout challenge

Running for your life

With running, more is not necessarily better.

Running for five to 10 minutes a day can help people live longer, an Iowa State University study found. Runners were likely to live three years longer than non-runners. Reduced mortality risks were the same among participants who ran for five to 10 minutes a day at a slow speed as among those who ran more than three hours a week.

If you've never exercised before, talk to your medical professional about how to get started safely.

Minutes tips to better health

- Ride your bike

- Do yoga

- Walk the dog

- Hop on an exercise bike or treadmill

- Climb stairs on your break

- Walk at a local park

- Run around the block

- Check out fitness apps and online classes

- Google 10-minute workouts — there are lots to choose from

- Compete in activity-based videogames

- Perform several rounds of body weight exercises (lunges, sit-ups and push-ups) while watching TV

- Have walking work meetings

- Perform child's pose and other stretches on a mat or towel

- Perform hip flexor stretch. (Google a few options.) They say the hips are the body's emotional junk drawers. It's amazing the movement in attitude that can come after freeing the hips.

Bite-sized bits

"The minute my legs begin to move my
thoughts begin to flow."
– Henry David Thoreau

"We don't stop playing because we grow old;
we grow old because we stop playing."
– George Bernard Shaw

"Whatever gets you moving and out of
your head is good for you."

"A year from now you may wish you had started today."
– Karen Lamb

"Exercise is king. Nutrition is queen. Put them together
and you've got a kingdom."
– Jack LaLanne

"Every workout counts. The only bad workout
is the one that didn't happen."

"When you feel like quitting, remember why you started."

"Motivation is what gets you started.
Habit is what keeps you going."

"No matter how slow you go you're
still lapping everyone on the couch."

Chapter 12

Over the years I've worked amid the literati, the glitterati and the shit-erati!

Bear with me. This isn't about to be an ego-fuelled brag fest about My Brilliant Career. I need to make an important point.

I had a long and interesting journalistic career. For example, I interviewed Great Train Robber Ronald Biggs in Rio de Janeiro and spent a couple of days hanging out with him. Like most of my colleagues, I've met prime ministers and pop stars and brave people gripped by tragedy, and had the honour of telling their stories.

I have pumped out a full-page column in Australia's biggest-selling newspaper, giving me an access-all-areas pass to global sporting events and opening nights. I've had my own radio segments. I've travelled to the Grand Slams and worked alongside my tennis heroes. I've slogged it out for years as a communications consultant.

I feel like an old tap dancer or hoofer. I've never missed a curtain call or a deadline and while I've made millions of missteps, I smear on the red lipstick, fix a smile, shuffle my feet and keep turning up.

Over the years I have seen people do all manner of things to derail their career — get blind drunk, hit on workmates, tell their boss what they really think of them.

*But after spending 40 years in the workforce, I honestly believe the worst thing you can do for your career is **get old**!*

Once your clock ticks past the age of 50 in the workplace, people start to treat you differently. Past 60? You're lucky if anyone even notices you're still there.

You've probably heard of the term mansplaining? When a man – but it can be a woman too – patronises you by oversimplifying something they're explaining to you.

Well, that's exactly what it feels like being over 50 in many work situations.

I'm calling it oldie-splaining.

I hear it when I'm speaking to head-hunters about roles that may be of interest. Or from a d*ckhead middle manager when they think they're being helpful but just showing they are a little bit more important than you. Or from that colleague who is trying to show you what to do as you fumble with the tech.

Yep. oldie-splaining. "Plug it into the M.O.D.E.M," they say slowly, deliberately and lots louder than needed.

"I am old, not deaf, you f-wit."

I admit that when the tech guy asks me "How many gigs?" I think he is referring to the number of rock bands I've seen recently. And a "browser"? That's me, as I poke around the shops looking for something to buy.

Don't even get me started on "software" packages!

Being an "older" person in the workforce can be a whole new level of outrageous.

*Yes, it's true I **am** hopeless at technology. Nope, I can't be fagged working 10-hour (or even eight-hour, if the truth be known) days any more.*

And I have about as much interest in playing office politics as I have in playing the pokies. I dream of climbing Mt Kilimanjaro, not some boring corporate ladder.

*But I do have experience, integrity, kindness, wisdom and **some** skills that are still relevant.*

However, regardless of our expertise, experience or energy, our perceived value has dried up. For older people in the workplace, our currency and cache has crumbled.

It's a scandal. Why is no one screaming about it?

It's an unspoken code. Jobs we should walk into suddenly evaporate, people stop directing their comments or questions to us in meetings, colleagues are less feverish about seeking us out at social events ...

And I politely pretend not to notice.

I might not have the same hunger as I once did. I certainly have different priorities, but I am far from lacking in ambition, energy or capability. I just want to do it differently, more modestly and gently than the younger corporate killer.

I am not playing in the centre or on the forward line any more, but I'm happy doing my bit for the team on the wing.

I still have something to give. I am happy to continue to contribute in a low-key role, while eking out a satisfactory salary or stipend.

It doesn't mean I expect to be treated as a lesser person or as stupid.

I've seen the prospects of lots of men I know shrivel up once they turn 50. Same, maybe even worse for women. Surplus to requirements.

One friend says the main reason she had a facelift was to make herself more employable. Another tells me she will never let her hair go grey while she's still working. Extreme maybe, but ...

Women are judged by how we look. And if that's old, shame on you and get ready for the consequences.

At the moment, I am working as a small part of a big team (these aren't the d*ckheads referred to earlier!) improving job opportunities for people with disabilities.

Thankfully our workplaces are getting so much better at being inclusive — and we hear, rightly, lots about removing barriers for people irrespective of sexual orientation, gender, mental illness, ethnicity, religious beliefs etc.

We are beginning to better understand the impact of unconscious bias and discrimination on these cohorts.

*But where is the outrage about the attitudes and treatment for **older** workers?*

Where is the "inclusion training" or the senior workers strategy? Where is the extra support or programs to assist older workers to learn the tech in a language, style and pace that suits — not one that freaks them out?

My close friend Janet and I reckon we should start our own movement.

Well, here it is, let's launch it. Maybe we should call ourselves OPADAWS? (Older People Against D*ckheads at Work). I'm open to suggestions.

Funnily enough, what's even more surprising about discrimination against older people is — unlike that related to gender, sexual orientation, race, challenged mental or physical health, ability level or social standing — we all have a vested interest.

The irony is ageing will happen to every single one of us if we're lucky enough to continue to breathe.

Actually, the ultimate act of change is ageing.

And there are a million things we can do to help ourselves age well. Many suggestions are here in this book. Pick the ones that serve you.

And let's do it together — disgracefully!

12 — Longevity & anti-ageing

*"It's important to have a twinkle
in your wrinkle."*

Every tick of that clock, every one of us is ageing. As I said, the ultimate act of change is ageing.

In our Western world, ageing is viewed by many as a little embarrassing, careless and messy. A misdemeanour. Believing that we still have lots to learn and contribute is a hardcore crime. Almost as bad as stealing. Or wearing blue and green without a colour in between.

Rather than believe our best years are still ahead, once we get to a certain age, we are expected to occupy less space, dress soberly, behave, be demure. And be dull.

If you're reading this thinking that you're too young to worry about it, sorry to say but our cognitive processes peak in our 20s. In fact, most of our body's systems are thought to climax between 18 and 30.

(Leon Flicker, professor of geriatric medicine at the University of Western Australia.)

It is a bit miserable to point out, but as we move through our world, we suffer little bits of damage — it could be from sunlight, bacteria, a sprained ankle, shonky DNA, bad food — that the body battles to repair.

But rather than be celebrated for our cumulative experience, wisdom and maturity, ageing is mostly not viewed as a positive at all. And much of this is because of the focus on our physical looks and how they are apparently in decline.

Yet history is full of fabulously inspiring people who never would have been asked to prance along a Victoria's Secret runway.

Beauty and anti-ageing "specialists" are skimming wealth from women's insecurity like fat off broth, while offering little more than a promise to try to help us look like everyone else (12).

The same applies to men, but statistically many more women are succumbing to pressure to eliminate the very qualities that give them character and make them unique. Pressure to smooth out the perceived "irregularities", resulting in uniformly stretched eyes, plumped-up cheeks, ironed foreheads and fully baked but perky breasts.

Social media has narrowed the definition of beauty to what can be photographed, filtered and posted, which neglects the essence, according to Australian author Julia Baird.

Beauty can be warmth, conversation, intelligence, charm or a certain grace or magnetism. And so much more. None of which is captured in a static photograph, she writes.

A quarter of how we age is determined by genetics, according to the World Health Organisation. And the rest comes down to lifestyle, socio-economic factors and attitude.

Yeah, yeah, we know. Smoking, poor diet, being overweight or obese and high blood pressure are key contributors. Any geriatrician will tell you a balanced diet and regular exercise are key to supporting positive ageing and, in turn, a longer life.

Stimulating our mind helps minimise disease risk. With our brains — just like our muscles — use it or lose it.

At a time when we are addicted to screens, filter our faces in selfies, exercise on machines and talk to recorded messages and robots, we wonder why there is so much anxiety, depression and disease.

Can there be any more powerful call to slow down, draw breath and go get ourselves a dose of perspective?

Like it or not, ageing continues happening every second of our life. The changes are neither in a straight line nor consistent, and as we know, there are huge differences between us in the speed and way we age.

But probably the best thing you can do for healthy ageing is just keep having a go. Stay engaged in life, do things you love, socialise, learn new skills, have a laugh.

Having a strong purpose boosts health and longevity. Finding meaning in life, especially when facing challenges, is key to resilience and survival.

The trick is to prioritise things you love. And then do them repeatedly.

Stand up tall and fill your space. Don't recoil. Find your voice and raise it. You've reached the age, whatever that may be, where you can reinvent your life, relationships and goals with renewed vigour.

We have a licence to be kinder to ourselves, not worry so much about what other people think of us and basically not give two f*cks any more.

We have well and truly earned our right to reject rejection.

Q & A

Question?

Have you ever thought someone was unattractive initially but changed your mind over time?

Answer

Nearly two-thirds of people in one study replied yes, saying their perception changed after getting to know a person better.

It's what's on the inside that counts

The red carpet is a cruel carnival (12).

Are we living in a galaxy where wrinkles are not a sign of maturity but of carelessness or lack of money?

Women are actually asking surgeons for "Instagram faces" that look like they've been filtered.

Many prominent women have pricked and plumped and tortured their faces because of criticism of those who show their age.

We see so many startled eyes, puffy lips, smooth foreheads, puffed cheeks, hoiked and enlarged breasts, thickets of eyelashes and giant hairy caterpillars of eyebrows that we have almost forgotten what beauty actually is.

This is happening, according to writer Julia Baird, because too many of us feel like failures the moment we look in the mirror before our day has even begun.

One of the biggest challenges as a mother of girls is working out how to stop them from frowning when they look in the mirror. How do we teach them to recognise the beauty of a whole person and not dice themselves into limbs, eyes, noses, thighs — bits they might decide "need fixing". (12)

Eighty-six per cent of women are not satisfied with their body and only two per cent would describe themselves as beautiful. The global beauty and youth-chasing industry is estimated to be worth US$534 billion.

Surely something is out of whack here?

I'm all for anyone taking steps that make them feel better. And I respect everyone's right to make the changes that feel appropriate for them. But I do suggest before you rush out and spend a fortune on a fab face fad you should take a few minutes for a deeper gaze within. Look beneath the surface.

It's worth questioning aspirational concepts of beauty, age and the products designed to help us achieve them. Let's be open to a more authentic, inclusive and affirming picture.

Certainly, do invest in a simple skin care routine including a good sunscreen. And remember one of the most effective anti-ageing options we have is exercise. Maybe try diving more into the ocean rather than the lotion or potions.

At least 26 common illnesses could be positively affected by exercise, including cardiovascular disease, type 2 diabetes, obesity, dementia, osteoarthritis, osteoporosis and some cancers, according to a 2015 study.

So maybe lose the need for Instagram likes and pageant ribbons. Let's change our lens to be gentle with ourselves and harsh to the forces that teach us to hate ourselves.

And in doing so, reject the idea that older ladies and men should just fade away and behave.

Exercise

When we look in the mirror, most of us zone straight to areas we believe to be flawed and imperfect. Every time you see your reflection force your gaze to one or more areas that you know — or have been told — are your best features. This could be your personality, a physical trait, your spirit, or another characteristic. Acknowledge them. Focus on them with gratitude. Do this as many times a day as you can for at least a week and compare how you feel about yourself.

Become a super-ager

Want to flourish later in life? When it comes to ageing well, genes, diet and lifestyle are clearly important, but researchers say we can upgrade the ageing process to "positive ageing" by making a few important behavioural changes. (17.) Having perspective helps you remember the past fondly while also looking ahead to the future. Many of the world's super-agers say they are better able to keep things in perspective, because they have more years to look back on and remember how they came through hard times.

If you fear dementia, the data is comforting. Recent studies show less than 20 per cent of over-85s suffer from the condition. So your risk is just one in five and there are plenty of lifestyle changes you can make to minimise it.

Benefits of ageing

We often care less about what other people think, which can be liberating. And there is a sense of peace that comes from understanding where you and the puzzle pieces of your life fit in.

Appreciation

Love your body and face for how they are.

Moving and grooving

Exercise improves muscle strength, balance, bone density and the immune, cardiovascular and respiratory systems. It boosts mood and supports brain and spinal health. Being active with people is important for cognitive stimulation.

Just a small amount of activity can make a meaningful difference, and resistance training is particularly important. There are cases where this has transformed once-bedbound patients in their 80s and 90s. Introduce incidental movement into your day — carry your shopping bags instead of using a trolley, walk instead of driving or tend to your garden.

Channel your envy into purpose

Comparing ourselves to others is a fruitless exercise that makes us feel, a) not enough or b) better than.

We all have our own timeframe. We all know the child protégé who didn't kick on. But there are plenty of people whose talents don't come to the fore until later in life.

- Fashion designer Vera Wang was a figure skater then a journalist before opening a bridal boutique at the age of 40-something

- Although Karl Lagerfeld pursued fashion from the age of 14, it was only later in life he transformed to reign as head designer at Chanel at the age of 82. At the age of 68 he lost 41kg as he wanted to wear the high fashion clothes he loved

- Celebrated actor Dame Judi Dench was 60 when her film career took off

- Samuel Jackson was 46 years old and a recovering cocaine and heroin addict when his acting career took off after he starred alongside John Travolta in Pulp Fiction

- Harlin Sanders, known as Colonel Sanders and the man behind KFC, didn't find success until he franchised his burgeoning chicken business at the age of 66

- At the age of 64, American author Diana Nyad became the first person to swim between Cuba and Florida without the protection of a shark cage.

Respecting ageing is one area where our Western societies have a lot to learn. In Aboriginal culture, an elder is someone recognised for their knowledge and ongoing contribution to their community, they are respected not neglected and are traditionally referred to as "Aunty" or "Uncle". Go for a walk in Beijing and you'll see the parks full of older people doing tai chi and dancing. There's no sense of people thinking: "I'm too old to do that."

Work out your "why" — blue zones

Dan Buettner discovered five blue zones where people live the longest and are healthiest, including Okinawa in Japan.

One key reason for the longevity of the women of Okinawa is their strong sense of purpose.

Okinawans are known for pursuing their *ikigai*, which means reason for being, or reason for waking up in the morning. (9)

National Geographic set out to find places which had a high concentration of 100-year-olds and clusters of people who had grown old without problems such as heart disease, obesity, cancer or diabetes.

- Ikaria, Greece, an island in the Aegean Sea with one of the world's lowest rates of middle-aged mortality and the lowest rates of dementia

- Okinawa, Japan, the largest island in a subtropical archipelago and home to the world's longest-lived woman at the time

- Ogliastra region, Sardinia, mountainous highlands on an Italian island that boasts the world's highest concentration of centenarian men

- Loma Linda, California, a community with the highest concentration of Seventh-day Adventists in the US where some residents live 10 more healthy years than the average American

- Nicoya Peninsula, Costa Rica, where residents have the lowest rates of middle-aged mortality and the second-highest concentration of male centenarians. (4)

Until recently, the diets in these regions consisted almost entirely of minimally processed plant-based foods — mainly whole grains, greens, nuts, tubers and beans. People ate meat, on average, only five times a month.

They mostly drank water, herbal teas, coffee and some wine. They drank little or no cows' milk.

Breaking bread

The Christians were on to something with the philosophy of "breaking bread" together. For people in the "Blue Zones" growing, preparing, serving and eating are all sacred practices with the power to bring families, homes, communities, values and their natural environment together in a daily rhythm.

Top 10 Minute Tips to change your life with food

- Cook at home to take control of your ingredients

- Make it taste good. Even long lives are too short if you don't like what you're eating!

- Share meals with family and friends. Double the ingredients and swap a pot!

- Give thanks and conduct a daily ritual to pause

- Hara hachi bu, which translates to eat until you are 80 per cent full. The Okinawans murmur these three words before they eat. Ikarians, Sardinians, Costa Ricans and Adventists all begin meals by saying a prayer. If you have no religious inclination, give gratitude

- When you eat alone, put your phone away, avoid reading, watching TV or jumping on your computer

- Enjoy and celebrate food. None of these rituals should feel like restriction or deprivation

- Balance is best. Pick one day a week and make it a celebratory day of a life well lived to splurge on a meal with your favourite foods.

How do I manage home cooking?

- Eat breakfast at home

- Pack your lunch the night before

- Prepare ingredients for dinner in the morning. Slow cooking is a great way to plan a Blue Zone dinner

- Shop and prepare meals for the week on the weekend and freeze.

A healthy diet is just one piece of the longevity puzzle, which also includes having a circle of lifelong friends, a sense of purpose, constant body movement and daily rituals to mitigate stress.

Legs up the wall

Lying on your back with your legs up the wall for 10 minutes has been hailed as an elixir of youth and miracle sleep cure. Traditional yoga teachings claim the pose can do everything from make "grey hairs and wrinkles inconspicuous" to "destroying old age and death". While the benefits won't be quite so magical, the pose can ease a range of ailments, including anxiety, headaches and insomnia. It's a perfect pose to help you unwind before bedtime.

Top 10 Minute Tips to change your life

Ten power longevity tips

Many residents of the original Blue Zones practise 10 healthy lifestyle habits that help them live longer, heathier, happier lives.

1. **Move naturally.** The world's longest-living people are constantly nudged into moving by their environment. Every trip to work, to a friend's house requires walking

2. **Purpose.** In Blue Zones, people say they have something to live for beyond work — the reason "why they wake up in the morning". Research shows a sense of purpose is worth up to seven years of life expectancy

3. **Less of the stress already.** Long-lived people have developed routines to shed stress. Okinawans take a few moments each day to remember their ancestors.

Adventists pray, Ikarians take a nap and Sardinians enjoy a happy hour

4. **80 per cent rule.** Japan's Okinawan Blue Zone people remind themselves to stop eating when their stomachs are 80 per cent full, with the phrase Hara hachi bu. If Americans, English people and Australians adopted this rule they could lose an average of 17 pounds or eight kilograms in the first year

5. **Plant slant**. Including fava beans, soy and lentils is the cornerstone of most centenarian diets, which also include relatively small amounts of meat

6. **Wine o'clock (yeah!).** People in all the Blue Zones (even some Adventists) drink alcohol moderately and regularly — one or two glasses a day with friends and food. Moderate drinkers tend to outlive non-drinkers

7. **Your tribe and vibe.** Social circles support healthy behaviour. Okinawans, for example, create moais — groups of five friends who are committed to each other for life

8. **Community.** Research has shown that attending spiritual or community services with those who share your values and beliefs four times a month adds four to 14 years of life expectancy. To some it may be a

community group, others a church, ashram, temple or sporting arena

9. **Loved ones first.** Successful centenarians in Blue Zones put their families and loved ones first. They invest time and love into their children and the children care for their elders. Having a life partner can add up to three years to life expectancy (4)

10. **Sleep.** In Blue Zones, most centenarians go to bed shortly after sunset and wake with daybreak. A half-an-hour nap is a daily ritual in many zones

11. **A relaxing bedtime routine is key.** No screens — including phones — in the bedroom

(Hypocrite alert! In the interest of full disclosure, I have written most of this book on my computer in my bed at all hours. Whoops. But it worked. I finished the book, in 10-minute increments, but my sleep patterns are all over the shop ☺)

In the Blue Zone of Ikaria, more than 80 per cent of people aged between 65 and 100 are still having sex! (And no little blue pills in sight).

Sex is also a verified longevity enhancer.

Top longevity foods from Ikaria, Greece	
The secrets of a Mediterranean diet:	
Olive oil	Chickpeas
Wild greens	Lemons
Potatoes	Mediterranean herbs
Feta cheese	Coffee
Black-eyed peas	Honey
Top longevity foods from Okinawa, Japan	
Okinawans over the age of 65 still enjoy the world's highest life-expectancy	
Bitter melon, known as goya	Brown rice
Tofu	Green tea
Sweet potatoes	Shitake mushrooms
Garlic	Seaweed (Kombu and Wakame)
Turmeric	
Top longevity foods from Sardinia, Italy	
Goat and sheep milk	Fava beans and chickpeas
Flat bread	Tomatoes
Barley	Almonds
Sourdough bread	Local red wine
Fennel	

Top longevity foods from Loma Linda, California	
Avocados	Water, six to eight glass a day
Salmon	Oatmeal
Nuts	Wholewheat bread
Beans	Soy milk
Top longevity foods from Nicoya Peninsula, Costa Rica	
Maze tortillas	Black beans
Squash	Bananas
Papayas	Peach palms
Yams	

Tips for career longevity

♦ Niches create riches. Specialise! Developing mastery in certain areas reduces the risk of mistakes and sets you apart from the crowd

♦ Always be learning. Keep your skills current by doing online and other courses

♦ Keep abreast of the tech. Technology is moving at an unprecedented pace, keep adapting

- Incorporate time in your day for reading. Become a regular reader of info in your industry

- Know your business. Understand your industry and how your company does business

- Self-care isn't just an out-of-office activity. If you want to be successful and enduring, look after yourself both at and away from work. Careers suck up so much time you might otherwise devote to your physical and emotional wellness, so use your breaks to walk in nature or write in your journal

- Be a brain to pick and an ear to listen. If you're not trying to climb the greasy pole yourself any more, you're much more ready to mentor and help other people

Bite-sized bits

"The quality, not the longevity, of one's life is what is important."
— Martin Luther King Jr.

"Your body hears everything your mind says."
— Naomi Judd

"Even I don't look like Cindy Crawford in the morning."
— Cindy Crawford

"I think your whole life shows in your face and you should be proud of that."
— Lauren Bacall

"Growing old is mandatory, growing up is optional!"
— Walt Disney

"We are always the same age inside."
— Gertrude Stein

"Getting old is like climbing a mountain; you get a little out of breath, but the view is much better!"
— Ingrid Bergman

"The best tunes are played on the oldest fiddles!"
— Ralph Waldo Emerson

"Anyone who keeps the ability to see beauty never grows old."
— *Franz Kafka*

"Focus on the parts of yourself that will not diminish with time — humour and wisdom are not like collagen. You will make more of them as you age."
— *Eleanor Gordon-Smith*

Chapter 13

— P.S. ... and then what happened?

The fish tacos are exceptional. The pinot noir, much better than average. He is not my normal type.

But there's something about him that I trust immediately.

Do I even need a boyfriend? Life as a middle-aged, single working mum is complicated and busy enough.

We are seated across from each other at a cute Mexican restaurant. It's our first date.

Blah, blah, blah, blah. Nerves sometimes cripple people's ability to speak. Sadly, I'm not one of them. Verbal dysentery. Blah. Blah. He gets a million points for laughing at all the right spots and showing (feigning?) interest.

It feels like we've known each other forever. We're the last people in the restaurant.

"*Tell me about your girls?*" *Michael asks me.*

"*They are incredible. I'm so proud of them. Yep, they are a handful but they have both had a rough ride,*" *I tell him.*

"*Tell me about your boys?*" *I ask.*

"*They are incredible. I'm so proud of them. Sure, they are a handful. You see ... they both live with disabilities.*"

There's a stab in my heart. It splits open the armour and out pours a lifetime of emotional nectar.

This is the moment that my life changes completely.

I look at him. And he at me.

And we both realise we will spend the rest of our lives together.

We've been a family for 10 years now.

It started inauspiciously with Raphaela and Romany, who were early teens at the time and definitely did not want any new man in our life. They dubbed him The Prick.

Fortunately, relations have improved since then and they love their stepdad a lot. They each add something previously missing in the other's life.

All four of our children are unique, with their own strengths and challenges.

Like the Japanese art form, we each bring gold veins that show where our pot has been broken and mended and reminds us that the former breakages can become something beautiful.

The damage and repair are part of our history, rather than something to disguise.

Raphaela and Romany are both doing well. Despite it all, they've emerged kind, caring, strong and decent people. They've graduated from university, have good jobs and are following their passions.

Finn and Zac, who both have autism and an intellectual disability, are also finding their own paths. Finn loves his iPad, going to the beach, the Wiggles, music and Michael Jordan. Zac is kind and joyous. He loves making people laugh, playing sport and his Australian rules football team, Geelong.

The boys teach all the people in their life, including their mum and stepfather, something profound every day. Sometimes it's as simple as gratitude or resilience or how to live in the moment.

Michael calls our family a happy hot mess. It sounds saccharine but he and I have finally found our soulmate. A better father and stepfather I'm yet to see.

We all know life is not just Pollyanna and picket fences. Shit gets real. Reality does bite. I won't lie, it's damn tough sometimes. And sometimes a gazillion affirmations or meditations or rituals aren't going to change how hard it is. But it does change how I turn up for it.

Like all of us, life has definitely pushed me to the edge. Which is why I have written — and believe in — this book.

Despite my enthusiasm, I am nervous putting *Change Your Life in 10 Minutes* out into the world. Who am I to challenge the pecking order? That little girl with big dreams still fears stepping out into judgment. Except this time there's no tennis racquet for protection.

Being vulnerable is uncomfortable. How do we fulfill our purpose and live truthfully — without drowning, reducing ourselves or sticking our neck out for the haters and the envious to chop straight off? It would be easier and safer to stay on the shore.

"You think you are so good don't you. Who do you even think you are? Why do you bother? You don't deserve success. Don't get too big for your boots, Missy."

Words have power. So I am finding mine.

I know I am a lot. When I talk, it's hard to stop. Over the years critics mistake this for ego and deliberately drawing attention to myself. I have a thousand ideas competing for space in my head and spilling out. (It could probably be ADHD but the only labels I've ever really investigated to date have been stamped on a fancy pair of stilettos.)

My need to connect and be heard is driven by a genuine passion, enthusiasm and eagerness to engage and help people.

I have learnt the hard way that it takes courage to be the people we came here to be.

When tested, I remember that initial feeling of impossibility and hopelessness when poking my little arms into the resistance of the ocean while swimming. Jerk, grind, jerk.

The tide turns to support me. The sun is rising. The staccato strokes start to smooth. Rhythm and momentum and direction flow my way. After the relatively simple act of pushing through, my sense of self is transformed. I feel fantastic.

(By the way, I made that swim around the island that I mentioned in Chapter 1. Who cares if it was jerk, grind, jerk. It might not have been elegant, but it was still motion, progress and an achievement to celebrate.)

My beautiful mum was the one who planted the important seed: Never, Ever, Give Up. Even when the pain is overwhelming, remember the one-percenters. If you can move just one inch you will get there.

Just get on with it, she'd always say. Have a crack. You have 10 minutes. Do something with it.

You might just change your life.

Appendix

100 random tiny things to get you moving

Just in case you haven't had enough 10 Minute tips or found one that works for you — here's my parting shot ... 😊

1.   Wake up at a reasonable time

2.   Make an appointment for something that will help your health or spirit

3.   Make a shopping list

4.   Meditate to quiet your thoughts. Browse YouTube for guided meditations or download apps like Headspace

5.   Try a brain teaser or quiz

6.   Take a virtual tour

7.   Read an interesting article

8.   Unsubscribe from unwanted email lists

9.   Doodle something cool

10.   Write a very short story

11.   Walk your dog if you have one

12.   Write a blog post

13.   Sleep an extra 10 minutes

14.   Tidy a room

15.   Watch the sunrise/sunset

16.   Read today's news

17.   Start dinner

18.   Plan your next holiday

19.   Write down your thoughts

20.   Update your calendar

21.   Clean out your junk drawer

22.   Search for new ideas for your next meal

23.   Unload the dishwasher

24.   Declutter your desk

25.   Organise your shoes into tidy rows of pairs

26. Pay bills

27. Change your sheets (see I told you it'd eventually change your life!)

28. Give yourself a mini manicure

29. Sort out your makeup bag

30. Start a garden

31. Clean weeds out of your yard

32. Set the table

33. Pick a bunch of flowers and create a beautiful vase

34. Sit quietly and listen

35. Make brownies

36. Sort through your emails

37. Call a friend

38. Squeeze a stress ball

39. Stretch

40. Dance like crazy to three songs

41. Run a kilometre

42. Do 25 squats

43. Go for a walk

44. Take a cat nap

45. Play with your or someone else's kids

46. Relax

47. Write a letter

48. Plan your meals for the next week

49. Walk up and down stairs

50. Open a dictionary and learn new words

51. Do a random act of kindness

52. Text three friends and say something nice

53. Delete apps you don't use

54. Go fishing

55. Shop online

56. Learn more about your industry

57. Do 10 push ups

58. Update your contact lists

59. Clean out rubbish from your car

60. Go grocery shopping

61. Plan an adventure

62. Check in on a friend

63. Get your finances in order

64. Do 10 minutes of household chores

65. Make a to-do list

66. Do 10 minutes of jobs on your to-do list

67. Go outside

68. Move your body

69. Explore healing aromas. Rosemary, lavender and sage can improve our moods. Put your favourite essential oils in a spray bottle with water

70. Listen to your intuition rather than try to think your way into happiness and freedom

71. Wash you face with cold water

72. Say sorry. It will free you

73. Send someone special an e-card

74. Think of someone you know who is struggling. Send them a kind message

75. Put a rubber band on your wrist to symbolise a change you want to make. Flick it when you need to remind yourself

76. Pick three things to delegate and politely assign them to others

77. Find recipes to make your own face masks

78. Google how different colours can impact your mood

79. Leave work at work

80. Give your CV a facelift

81. Give your face a "facelift": A 10-minute cleanse, tone and mask routine

82. Photograph your mementos to get rid of clutter you're finding hard to let go of

83. Eat slower. It's better for your health and digestion

84. Give up nagging — give your relationship a lift

85. The quickest supermarket queue is always behind the fullest trolley (greeting, paying and packing take longer than you think)

86. Plant spring bulbs, even if they're just in a pot

87. Set aside 10 minutes a day to do something you really enjoy

88. Laugh shamelessly at your own jokes

89. Take the stairs

90. Be polite to rude strangers — it's oddly thrilling

91. Say hello to your neighbours

92. Drop your shoulders and stand tall

93. Keep a book in your bag to avoid mindless scrolling

94. Make a friend from a different generation

95. Don't save things for best. Wear, use and enjoy them today

96. Learn some popular moves. Download TikTok and challenge yourself to learn a trending dance

97. Give knitting a try. There's a reason it's a favourite of grandmas — it is very calming

98. Call a relative and get an old family recipe to try

99. Write a bucket list — list everything you want to do before you die

100. Start now.

Create our own 10 Minute tribe

Nothing would make me happier than to know that even one single tip — one miserly 10 minutes — has made a difference in your life.

So please let me know. I would truly love to hear from you. I would also appreciate hearing the tips that have worked for you.

Join our community

Website: www.changeyourlifein10mins.com

Email: www.changeyourlifein10minutes.com

Follow us on Instagram: changeyourlifein10mins

*"Start where you are.
Use what you have. Do what you can."
— Arthur Ashe*

Acknowledgements

A big thanks to my 10 Minute tribe of readers and supporters whose feedback has been invaluable:

- Joanne Anderson
- Lucy Niall
- Michael O'Connell
- Dr Tom Manolitsas
- Tanya Preston
- Raphaela
- Romany
- Rosemary O'Connell
- Christine Acquroff
- Annie Glasson
- Michelle Michie
- Kathee Gunn
- Amy Vanrijthoven
- Pamela Michie
- John Michie
- Paulie Stewart (whom I played in the final of the under 9's!)
- Kathee Gunn
- Denise Michie
- Pablo Campillos
- Rowena Stocks
- Joanna Halley
- Di Guiney
- Sonja Leon
- Janet Coningsby
- Jacki Mitchell

- Nadika Gerber
- Chantelle Sturt
- Louise Ajani
- Mandy Engelhardt
- Kath Lombard

- Andi Armstrong
- Anna Betts
- Giorgio Liapakis
- Alessia Spicuglia
- Ruby Lewis

References

1. Tiny Habits, Why starting small makes lasting change easy, BJ Fogg PhD, Penguin 2020

2. Change Your Life, Zoe Bosco, Affirm, 2022

3. The Resilience Project, Hugh Van Cuylenburg, Penguin, 2019

4. Blue Mind, Wallace J. Nichols, Little Brown, 2014

5. Blue Spaces, How & Why Water Can Make You Feel Better, Dr Catherine Kelly PhD, Wellbeck Balance, 2021

6. Atlas of the Heart, Brene Brown, Penguin Random House, 2021

7. Liptember 2022 research (https://raisely-images. imgix.net/liptember-foundation/uploads/ liptember-foundation-2022-research-the-

mental-health-gender-gap-understanding-
womens-mental-health-in-australia-final-lr-pdf-
6c2d40.pdf)

8. 10 Mindful Minutes, Goldie Hawn, Perigree Books,
    2011

9. National Geographic. Discovering Blue Zones Dan
    Buettner. Bluezones.com, 2005

10. Purpose, Lisa Messenger, 2021

11. Guide to Wellbeing, Katherine Wright, Geddes &
    Grosset, 2004

12. Phosphorescence, Julia Baird, Fourth Estate,
    2020

13. How Water Makes You Happier, More Connected
    and Better at What You Do, Little Brown, 2014

14. The Body Keeps the Score: Brain, Mind, and Body
    in the Healing of Trauma, Bessel van der Kolk M.D,
    Viking Press, 2014

Helpful websites & articles

General

https://www.nytimes.com/2021/05/18/well/pandemic-wellness-exercise.html

https://www.mentalhealth.org.uk/explore-mental-health/statistics/stress-statistics

https://jamanetwork.com/journals/jamainternalmedicine/fullarticle/2788473

https://www.sciencedaily.com/releases/2017/12/171221122543.htm

https://www.medicalnewstoday.com/articles/280279

http://guidetoself.com/anger-tips/#

https://www.oecd.org/coronavirus/policy-responses/tackling-the-mental-health-impact-of-the-covid-19-crisis-an-integrated-whole-of-society-response-0ccafa0b/

https://www.theage.com.au/lifestyle/
life-and-relationships/how-do-we-age-
and-can-we-delay-it-20211004-p58wzy.
html?utm_source=HouseDisplay&utm_
medium=HouseInventory&utm_
campaign=Explainer&utm_content=Explainer_
Miniscroller

https://cbtprofessionals.com.au/the-7-cs-of-resilience/

https://www.rwjf.org/en/blog/2014/08/loneliness a
signif.html (Loneliness and smoking).

https://news.gallup.com/poll/246200/gallup-national-
health-index-work.aspx

https://blogs.scientificamerican.com/observations/
loneliness-is-harmful-to-our-nations-health/

https://theimportantsite.
com/10-reasons-why-community-is-important/

https://www.tech21century.com/the-human-brain-is-
loaded-daily-with-34-gb-of-information/

https://www.the-next-tech.
com/blockchain-technology/
how-much-data-is-produced-every-day-2019/

https://www.mentalhealth.org.uk/
explore-mental-health/kindness/
kindness-matters-guide

https://www.lifehack.org/604180/why-changing-for-
the-better-isnt-as-difficult-as-it-seems

https://campushealth.unc.edu/
health-topic/10-ways-to-love-your-body/

https://guidetoself.com

https://jamesclear.com/marginal-gains

https://www.nytimes.com/2019/03/25/smarter-living/
why-you-procrastinate-it-has-nothing-to-do-with-self-
control.html

https://www.betterup.com/blog/
what-is-languish-how-to-flourish?hsLang=en

Water

http://www.saltyfit.com.au/why-swim-in-salt-water/

https://www.sonima.com/fitness/healing-water/

https://www.medicaldaily.com/benefits-cold-showers-7-reasons-why-taking-cool-showers-good-your-health-289524

Float Nation documentary on benefits of flotation tanks: https://www.youtube.com/watch?v=nHnbKjQGhHw

https://autismswim.com.au/2019/08/18/some-of-the-many-benefits-of-swimming-and-aquatic-therapy-for-those-with-asd-other-abilities/

https://www.autismparentingmagazine.com/benefits-swimming-autistic-children/

Mindfulness & breath

https://www.betterup.com/blog/mindful-breathing

https://www.mindful.org/3-minute-mindfulness-practice-ground-moment/

https://www.youtube.com/watch?v=ZToicYcHIOU

Resilience

https://www.apa.org/topics/resilience/guide-parents-teachers

https://www.verywellmind.com/
find-a-support-group-meeting-near-you-69433

https://cbtprofessionals.com.au/the-7-cs-of-resilience/

Connection

https://www.forbes.com/sites/
forbescoachescouncil/2017/04/13/
the-importance-of-aligning-your-values-with-your-
relationships/?sh=77a9fa94e4d1

https://www.tonyrobbins.com/mind-meaning/
how-to-raise-your-standards/

https://www.tonyrobbins.com/stories/
date-with-destiny/beliefs-create-world/

https://www.ncbi.nlm.nih.gov/pmc/articles/
PMC3150158/

Environment & greenspace

https://www.sciencedaily.com/
releases/2018/07/180706102842.htm

https://shedefined.com.au/wellbeing/struggle-to-wake-up-always-tired-how-to-improve-your-sleep/

https://www.lifecoach.com/articles/simplify-clutter/tips-to-clean-out-clutter/

https://www.lifecoach.com/articles/simplify-clutter/does-your-clutter-have-a-hidden-message/

https://www.huffpost.com/entry/benefits-of-making-your-bed_b_7980354

Words & affirmations

https://goop.com/wellness/mindfulness/the-scary-power-of-negative-words/

https://inspiregoodvibes.com/blogs/news/how-to-start-journaling#Types_Journaling\

Nourishment & weight management

https://www.health.qld.gov.au/news-events/news/good-mood-food-how-food-influences-mental-wellbeing-anxiety-depression-stress

https://www.healthier.qld.gov.au/food/

https://www.elitedaily.com/life/loving-body-inside-crucial-wellbeing/905717#:~:text=The%20%22love%20your%20body%22%20movement,cracks%20and%20tear%20you%20down

https://www.heysigmund.com/the-remarkable-power-of-touch/

https://greatergood.berkeley.edu/article/item/hands_on_research

https://www.ama.com.au/sickly-sweet/whats-the-problem

https://www1.racgp.org.au/newsgp/clinical/health-snapshot-of-the-'typical-australian'

https://www.afr.com/politics/federal/less-than-7pc-of-australians-eat-a-healthy-diet-20221020-p5bre6

https://www.theguardian.com/society/2022/may/19/more-than-42m-uk-adults-will-be-overweight-by-2040

Movement

https://itstimetexas.org/can-10-minute-workouts-really-improve-your-health/

https://www.wholelifechallenge.com/why-10-minutes-of-exercise-per-day-is-enough-to-get-you-results/

https://moffitt.org/endeavor/archive/10-minutes-of-exercise-could-save-lives/

https://www.healthline.com/health-news/moderate-vigorous-exercise-boosts-fitness-3-times-more-than-walking

https://archive.hs.iastate.edu/news/2014/07/28/iowa-state-professor-finds-leisure-running-reduces-mortality-risk/

https://www.newscientist.com/article/mg25033350-400-how-the-way-you-move-can-change-the-way-you-think-and-feel/

https://www.nytimes.com/2021/05/18/well/pandemic-wellness-exercise.html

Longevity & anti-ageing

https://www.ncbi.nlm.nih.gov/pmc/articles/PMC3827458/

https://positivepsychology.com/emotional-resilience/